The Ultimate Guide on What to Do When Someone You Love Dies

By Laurie Mueller, M.Ed

The Ultimate Guide on What to Do When Someone You Love Dies, First Edition

Dedicated to my mother, Helen (1913 – 1997),

Who told me to let my voice be heard.

Your pain is the breaking of the shell that
encloses your understanding.

Even as the stone of the fruit must break, that its heart may
stand in the sun, so must you know pain.

And could you keep your heart in wonder at the daily
miracles of your life, your pain would not seem less
wondrous than your joy;

And you would accept the seasons of your heart, even as
you have always accepted the seasons that
pass over your fields.

And you would watch with serenity through the
winters of your grief.

- Kahlil Gibran

Table of Contents

Update 2020: Introduction to the New Edition

The world has changed in this year of 2020, we hope temporarily. Some of the practices that we have used in the past are not practical or allowed. Meeting in groups can be dangerous and yet it is our nature as human beings to crave the company of others. How fortunate that we live in the age of the internet.

To buy this book, you pushed a button on your computer, tablet or phone screen. You read it on screen or ordered in paperback. And now, for meeting people 'in person', we have programs like Skype, Zoom and Facetime. We gather together virtually through the power of computing.

With the exception of some re-formatting for a new way of distributing books, I have left the content as it was originally written in 2009. The information is still important and relevant today. The difference is not in that we don't come together, but in how it has changed in how we come together.

We all live in hope that we will one day, in the not-to-distant future, return to a way of life where we can come together, shake hands, hug and kiss as we greet each other.

And so, I offer this book to you, in a time when I think there are people who need this guide more than ever. I send it out with love, and I hope that you will find comfort in some small way.

I hope you will share it with others who may need this help.

I look forward to any feedback you have by visiting the Author's Page of my website at https://lauriemconsulting.com

"In the wake of death we find solace and go on living."

Someone you love has just died. The first few days following the death are overwhelming. You feel dazed and numb and you wonder how you will deal with all the details associated with your loved one's death. When my mother died, I cried, I didn't sleep, I wrote a long tribute to her (which I later condensed and used as her eulogy) and then I wondered "What do I do now?" I went to the nursing home where she had lived, and I asked them "What do I need to do?" Somehow, I found the right steps to take because the nursing home staff, the funeral home staff, the church staff, the lawyer as well as my family and my friends were all there to support and guide me. I hope this guide will help you do the things you need to do in order to get through this very difficult time of your life.

Attitudes and customs for the memorialization of a deceased person have changed over the past few decades and we are still in a time of transition. It was only three decades ago that the deceased was embalmed and laid in a coffin in North America. Cremation was not usually an option. Depending on the person's religion, the body might have been set in a room for viewing for several days before the funeral service. A funeral service was held within the week of death and that service was completely officiated by the minister or funeral director. The service was often short – 30 minutes – and although brief facts about the deceased were stated, it was not the celebration of life that we are seeing these days. It was more of a religious observance than a celebration of a person. Once the service was completed, a car procession (with headlights on) followed the funeral car (called a hearse) with the casket inside and often family members led the way to the cemetery. Once at the cemetery, a graveside service was held as the body in the coffin was lowered into the ground. Stemming from Jewish tradition, a symbolic shovel of dirt was cast into the grave. We still see scenes like this in melodramas on television today. A reception followed and was held either in a home or a hall.

In services to memorialize our deceased love ones in this new century, we tell their stories. We play or sing their favorite songs and we flash pictures of their life on screens at the front of the room. The whole event is often choreographed by the family, or by the funeral director or minister. The ideal length of time for such a service is 45–60 minutes but overzealous family and friends who all want to contribute can lengthen the service. Some services have been known to go on for 2–4 hours! Refrigeration and cremation have eliminated the need to have a service within seven days. The service can take place when and where it is suitable for the family and friends. In some cases, this can take place weeks or even months after the death.

With the advent of a more multicultural lifestyle, a variety of customs are being incorporated into our memorials. This book is a guideline and I encourage you to be creative and meaningful when honoring your loved ones.

Whether you are working with a minister or funeral director, it is important for you to listen to their questions and to give them as much information as possible to help them create the right service.

Whether you are prepared or not, the loss of a loved one is difficult. This guide will help you get through this difficult time and to help you think about what will happen in the instance of your own death so that others will not be left unprepared.

Even though you have short notice, do not hurry your decisions. Do not settle on the first funeral home that you find or call the one that you attended for a service because it is the only name you know. Get information from as many sources as you can before making decisions without overwhelming yourself. Once you have decided on a venue, their professional staff will provide excellent help in your decision-making process.

The funeral director plays an important role in the process. Not only can you hire the funeral home director to coordinate the service, but it is also their job to prepare the body, to cremate or bury, to arrange for the Death Certificates and any other official duties that are needed at this time.

Support systems are important, and you should not be without them. Allow people to help. I read in the Reader's Digest many years ago about a man who knew how to help when one of his friends or neighbors died. He would polish the shoes of the family so that when they attended the funeral their shoes were shining. People will want to help you even if it is a little task that you need done. Perhaps a neighbor drops by and asks what they can do. You could ask them to cut the lawn. When my children's father died I was living 500 miles from them. My best friends said, "We will drive you to your children" and they did. I sat in the backseat as if it was a limousine and no one worried that I would get there safely in my distraught state.

The Reverend Bill Cantelon uses this in some of his eulogies:

We are here to share this profound sense of loss together.

From wisdom literature of past centuries we have the truth: "this is our grief and we must bear it." Our loved one's death brings a deep sense of loss; a loss beyond words. We must always realize the value of tears in expressing our loss. Through our tears we express our anger and hurt and with our tears we are moved toward healing. But we must always be mindful that we don't bear our loss alone. The Greek word "sympathos" means "to suffer together" and from the Latin we have the word "confortis" which means "to be made strong together. Combine these two words "sympathy and comfort" we have suffering together we are made strong together!" It is one of the strange paradoxes of life but true to experience.

Our friends help us carry our grief; many have said "I couldn't have made it on my own, without family and friends!"

God, of course, is always with us and helps us bear our loss. We are never alone.

Thanks for God's help and love and support and that which we receive from family and friends." (Rev. Bill Cantelon, personal communication, 24 April 2009)

This guide will help you to go through all the items that you will need to do or to delegate.

This is the time to pull all your organizational skills – learned and innate – together to help you get through this painful and stressful time.

Don't rely on your memory.

Write things down.

Make lists. I would even recommend that you carry a little pad of paper and pen around with you in your pocket so that you can list things as you think of them for future reference.

Keep a calendar.

Keep a journal that you can write in when you have something that you want to say or want to remember. For some people this will help you sort out feelings over this period in your life.

The 4D's – "Do – Delegate – Delay – Dump" – Management System will come in very handy at this time. There are a number of things that I have listed below that are important for you to "Do" or "Delegate" to others. I would suggest that everything else in your life can either be "Delayed" or "Dumped".

Chapter 1: What Do I Do Now? – A Practical Guide to Get You Through the First Days.

We understand death for the first time when
he puts his hand upon one whom we love.
Madame de Stael

1. Read through this entire list before beginning to do anything. By doing so, you will see the big picture and it will help you to determine how and when you need to begin. This is not a list for the executor, who is the person or institution named in a will by the deceased to distribute their assets and pay their bills after their death. Duties of an executor are not covered in this guide. When a person dies, their doctor or the local coroner must be notified. In some cases, the local police will also be notified. If you are with a person when they die, depending on the circumstances, get in touch with your local authorities and they will direct you.

2. Arrange for care for children, elderly spouse, and pets.

3. If the person lived alone: clean out the fridge; arrange a hold on their mail; cancel the telephone and cable; water the plants.

4. Make sure their home is secured from vandals or burglars.

5. Gather a support system around you. Accept help from others and allow yourself to be looked after. Your strength will come not just from within but with the help of those who love you.

6. Notify family, friends and business associates about the death. Delegate as much of this as you can to people in your support system. Include notification of:

   a. Relatives and friends (don't forget email and social media contacts)
   b. Employer
   c. School
   d. Solicitor
   e. Accountant
   f. Executor
   g. Home support agency
   h. Landlord
   i. Membership organizations

7. Discuss with family members any decisions that must be made. One person will need to make the final decision based on the input from the discussion.

8. If media has become involved in this death because of its suddenness or the fame of your loved one, delegate someone in your support system to handle the press and media.

9. Look after yourself. Take all the time that you need to rest, to exercise, to be alone with your thoughts or to

talk to others about your feelings. Allow yourself to cry, wail and gnash your teeth!

10. Locate the will, codicils (additions to the will) and trusts. Check the will for any requests regarding final arrangements. Locate life, health, auto and property insurance policies, and locate the safety deposit box.

11. Make sure that you have this information at your fingertips:

    a. Deceased's full name at the time of death
    b. Any names previously used (including maiden name)
    c. Date and place of birth
    d. The address, telephone and email address of the deceased at the time of their death and length of time at current address
    e. Occupation and title; name and address of current business or employer
    f. Date of marriage, if applicable
    g. Full name, occupation and date of birth of surviving partner, if applicable
    h. Names of mother and father and their birthplaces; mother's maiden name
    i. Whether or not the deceased was receiving government benefits such as pension or disability payments

12.	Locate these documents for use in the next few days:

  a.	Social Insurance (Security) Number (your country's government issued number)
  b.	Health Insurance or Service Number (again the name is dependent on your country)
  c.	Birth Certificate or particulars
  d.	Citizenship papers (if applicable)
  e.	Marriage Certificate (or particulars such as date)

13.	Within the first five days after death, you will need to decide which funeral home you will be using. The deceased may have already left directions. If the deceased had a pacemaker, let the funeral home know.

14.	Determine if the deceased belonged to a burial or memorial society that may make special arrangements for the funeral, such as military honor guards.

15.	Contact a clergy person or funeral director to help you prepare the service.

  a.	Contact several funeral homes if preplanning was not done by the deceased to find the best cost and most appropriate services for you. Be diligent and check around before making this major purchase for your loved one. You may choose to visit the home and interview the staff before making your decision. Sometimes when a person is emotional, rational decision making is harder to accomplish. Do not overspend on such items as the casket, the services offered, and the burial plot.

    b. Contact your church, if desired, as soon as possible and arrange a meeting.

16. If no arrangements were made beforehand by the deceased, make decisions on the following items:

    a. Cremation or burial
    b. Cemetery lot location and which space to open
    c. Memorial type and inscription
    d. Casket type
    e. Vault or sectional crypt

17. Sign necessary papers for burial permit.

18. Choose the clothing for the deceased and deliver to the funeral home. Include shoes and socks.

19. Decide when the funeral or memorial service will take place. Setting the service date will also depend on other activities happening in that location. Be aware that you may need to change your choice of time or move the service.

20. Select scripture, music and other details for the service along with the officiant. For more details see the Planning a Funeral or Memorial Service section of this guide.

21. Select pallbearers if the casket will be at the funeral.

22. Decide if you want to accept flowers. Decide if you would prefer people donated to a charitable organization that had meaning for the deceased. Have someone check out the information you will need to tell people and include the request in the obituary notice.

23. Write the obituary.

24. Write the eulogy or ask someone appropriate to write and present the eulogy. Provide information to the eulogist regarding facts and interesting stories.

25. Decide on clothing to wear to the funeral/memorial service for yourself and family.

26. Keep track of all donations, flowers, and cards received.

27. Attend to any transportation needs of family members for the service and include planning the funeral car list, if applicable.

28. Notify government agencies that send checks to the deceased.

29. Notify the executor of the will; if there is no will, decide on who in the family will sort matters out. A person who dies intestate (without a will) will have the government take charge of how their assets will be divided. In most areas this does not mean that they will

keep the assets, only that they will decide how the assets are divided and who they will be awarded to. They will also keep a fee for this service. Various countries and regions have their own policies. If there is no will:

    a. Decide who will apply to sort out the deceased's affairs

    b. In the UK, contact the Probate Registry to apply for 'letters of administration'

30. Make sure you have located and put in one spot all the deceased's important papers including: bank books; bill of sale for automobile(s) owned by the deceased; all property deeds; income tax returns; receipts; cancelled checks.

31. Arrange for cemetery burial or cremation services with the funeral home that you have chosen.

32. Keep records of the expenses you incur for the funeral, memorial services and related charges.

33. Watch out for people who prey upon bereaved families. There are people who look for death notices and make unfounded claims against the deceased. Some may also attempt to burglarize the home during the funeral service. Be cautious about such matters; have someone stay at the home during the funeral service and do not easily accept the claims of unknown individuals who lack documentation.

34. Order death certificates needed to inform government and other organizations of the death. See guidelines in the How to Write an Obituary section.

35. Close the accounts of the deceased. In some cases you will be asked to supply a death certificate. These may include:

   a. Bank accounts (Although bank accounts are frozen until the will is executed, you will need to inform the bank of the death.)
   b. Charge accounts
   c. Magazine and newspaper subscriptions
   d. Agreements
   e. Payments
   f. Direct debits

36. Cancel or change insurance details.

37. Contact the Life Insurance Company. They will need to be notified before starting the process of payment. This will not be immediate – expect a delay.

38. Notify:

   a. Relevant Tax Office
   b. Passport Office
   c. Drivers Licensing Agency
   d. Car Registration/change of ownership
   e. Utility Companies
   f. Dentist and other professional service providers

g. Trade unions, associations, and cancel membership

39. Note: *In the case of a spouse's death, it is helpful if organizations and institutions that may have this person on a phoning list be notified. This will help stop unwanted telephone calls that ask for the deceased.*

40. Protect the deceased's tangible property, such as silverware, dishes, furniture, or artwork. Later on, the next of kin and the executor will need to have these items appraised and distributed according to the deceased's wishes. This may be a difficult task if family and friends have already taken some items. The executor is responsible for distribution.

41. Donate medical aids such as hearing aids, eyeglasses, wheelchairs, walkers and pacemakers to organizations that can recycle and reuse these.

42. Write thank you notes to those who helped and supported you through this time; include friends, funeral director, clergy, music people, etc. Your words can be simple or not depending on your comfort level with writing. Simply "Thank you for your support and service in our time of sorrow" can be enough.

43. Clothing and other personal effects that need to be sorted by you should be done at a time when it feels right for you. Make sure that you have a friend or family member either present or on call if you need

their help or support. Do not do it when someone else tells you too, but when it feels right for you.

44.	Make any necessary changes to your will if it has been affected by the loss of this loved one.

This material is not intended to replace the advice of a qualified professional such as lawyer, funeral director, or accountant. Before making any commitment regarding the issues discussed here, consult with the appropriate professional.

A note about email contacts: I have received emails from the account of a deceased friend with a notification of their death written by a family member. Although this can be very effective to reach people in other cities or parts of the country that otherwise might not know or find out, be careful how you word the email. In some cases, sending the obituary notice through the email may be helpful.

Chapter 2: Planning the Funeral or Memorial Service

The Funeral is getting a makeover as a growing number of Americans have begun thinking outside the box, so to speak, about how they want to say Good-Bye to their loved ones. Not for them the weepy, organ-heavy ceremonies of the parents and grandparents. Funerals today are less about mourning a death than about celebrating a life.

Takeuchi Cullen

Funeral Service or Memorial Service

Definition: A ceremony or service held to honor a deceased person and a rite of passage for family and friends can be known by many names. When a casket with a body (either open or closed) is present and takes place within a week of the death, the service is typically known as a *funeral*. A *memorial service* may take place at any time. There may be more than one *memorial service* in a number of locations. The body is not present. Although a *funeral* typically takes place in a funeral home or in a religious location such as a church, a mosque, or a synagogue, a *memorial service* can take place in a funeral home, a religious location, a hall, someone's home, or even in a park-like setting.

A *celebration of life* is another name for a *memorial service.*

In this guide I will be focusing on the western Christian-based Protestant customs unless otherwise stated: I am only discussing the funeral and the memorial service, although there may be viewings, wakes, and graveside services that are also a part of your culture and customs.

As a minister in a Christian Church, Reverend Wilson was getting ready to prepare a funeral service and asked the bereaved family members if there was anything special they wanted her to do. The daughter said, "Yes, take out all mention of Jesus."

Note: If you decide to have the funeral or memorial service in a church, it is important that you agree with the faith of that church. Make sure where you choose has the same beliefs and faith that is in keeping with your beliefs and faith (or that of the deceased). If you do not want God mentioned in the service, use a funeral home or private hall rather than a church.

Planning the Service

Choose a funeral home:

- Check to see if the deceased has left instructions or a pre-arranged plan.
- Check out several before deciding; interview several either by phone or in person.

12

- Consider price, reputation, services available, facilities, and location.
- Do not be afraid to ask for a price list.
- Ask friends and family for references of funeral homes they may have used.
- Decide if you are going to have the service at the funeral home or in a church of your religious beliefs.
- Decide on the place and type of reception afterwards.

Once you have decided, talk to the funeral director or religious leader and discuss:

- Time
- Date
- Place
- Officiant
- Details of the service

Time and Date

You may have to be flexible with your time to accommodate out-of-town guests or other services that are taking place at the location of your choice.

Place

Some people use a public space such as a park. Check with the owners or managers of the space for permits or costs, and whether you need to book the time. You do not want to be kicked out of a space at an inopportune moment.

A public service for an unexpected death often attracts many mourners and this should be taken into consideration when planning a service of this type. Some families welcome this outpouring of sentiment at the funeral or memorial service. Others prefer a more private and intimate funeral service. This can be followed by a public memorial service planned by close friends and held some days later in a suitable location. Discuss your options and preferences and make a decision with which you are most comfortable.

Remember that churches have operating expenses and there will be a fee for their services as well. Soccer clubs, restaurants, and other places where the deceased had an affiliation are also used as service venues. *Remember there are costs associated with all things – don't expect anything to be free.*

Officiant

Your choices are broad for the person who will lead the service: a funeral director, a religious leader, a family member or friend.

If you decide to have the service in your home, you will still need to check with the funeral director to define what you can do and what they need to legally do in your area such as providing the burial or cremation certificate. A general rule is that there will be some requirements for a funeral (because you are dealing with a body), but a memorial service (because there is no body) does not require any legal documentation.

Details of the Service

These will be worked out with the officiant and you can use this guide to help you.

The first question the officiant may ask is whether you want a big public event, a small public event, a graveside service or a home service.

It is important to work with the person who will be leading the service and make sure that they have all the correct facts and pronunciation of the name, etc. Nothing is more disconcerting to mourners than to hear their loved one's name being mispronounced or being told a story about the deceased that is not true or not applicable to their life.

When Ted's grandmother, Anita, died the family listened as the young funeral director told stories about Anita's early years of marriage and they were surprised. "That wasn't right. Grandma never carried water or chopped firewood. Grandpa did that. Grandma always bragged about what a good husband he was!"

A Word about Children

Be sure to include the children in your planning and in everything you do. It is important that the children have the opportunity to mourn publicly.

Ushers

Have ushers to greet guests as they arrive. An usher could be a friend or relative, or a member of the funeral home staff. Their job is to:

- Greet people
- Assure guests they are in the right place
- Distribute programs
- Guide people to the guestbook

Guest Book

Many people like to know who has attended and have a record. A guest book is often placed at the front door for people to sign as they arrive.

The funeral home may supply one or you may choose to bring your own. It can be located close to the door at both the viewing and the funeral or memorial service.

Basket for Cards

A basket to collect sympathy cards can also sit close by the guest book.

Memorabilia and Picture Presentations

Focus people's attention on the front of the room. A large framed picture (at least 8 ½ x 11 inches) of the deceased will give the mourners a good visual experience. It is fairly inexpensive in most places to take an ordinary picture and have it enlarged on a color photocopy machine. You can then buy a frame or use a frame from something in your house.

You can have this display as people walk in, at the front of the room or in the reception area. Speak with the funeral director or minister and they will advise you. If you are having the service in your own home or in a rented hall, choose a place where people can gather to view the pictures and memorabilia and chat to each other about what they see. Those who attend the service appreciate this type of display. It gives them a conversation starter and helps people feel more at ease to talk amongst each other.

Add memorabilia to sit around the picture. People can view these items before and after the service and focus their gaze on them throughout the service. As for memorabilia – you will have a good idea of the kinds of things that were important to your loved one. Some items that I have seen – a canoe that my friend had built was carried in and placed at the front of the church (fortunately the doors were big enough for it to fit and he had been well known in the church and no one minded his canoe paying a visit!)

In the past, people have simply put out photo albums or put together a collection of photos to show. If you are putting together a physical photo presentation you can do so by displaying pictures on a table, in frames or in photo albums or binders, you can create a bulletin board or collage on poster board or you can create a digital presentation.

Helen was a very smart dresser and had quite a collection of hats that she wore as often as she could. Her daughter placed her purple hat at the front of the room beside the picture of her mother wearing the same hat. It brought a smile to many.

Some people display military medals. Another funeral had a sampling of the quilts that the deceased had made in her lifetime. One woman did have her laptop displayed and her grandchildren laughed when I talked to them about it because they said, "Grandma was the e-mailing queen!"

Marie told me that when she dies, she wants pictures of her Facebook account posted at the front of the room. She lives hundreds of miles from the rest of her family and that is how they keep in touch.

The Program

This handout for everyone who attends can either be an order of service or a tribute to the deceased. If you are working with a funeral director or clergy person, they will advise you on what they have to offer.

If you choose to print a program, it should include the components listed below, as well as an invitation to the reception afterwards. This will put people at ease and allow them to focus on their time of goodbye.

Components of a Service

Regardless of the type of service or the location and whether it is religious or non-religious, the following components are a good guide to follow:

- Greeting and Welcome
- Music (recorded, live, hymn or song)
- Readings (scripture, poetry, inspirational prose)
- Eulogies/Reflections (including picture presentations)
- Meditation/Prayer
- Closing

Length of a Service

How long should a service be? People prefer to attend for 45 minutes. I have heard stories of half an hour to 2 hours. Believe me; sitting for 2 hours is not an honor! You can visit for that long but keep the service tight at 45 minutes. When you have only 30 minutes, it may seem to others that you have not given sufficient time and attention to honoring the deceased. One minister told me about a funeral in which they honored two cultures and two religions in the service. By the time the church service and the graveside service had been completed the total time was 4 hours. Some people had to leave before it was over due to other commitments.

In some areas of the world this will not be a question – it will either be your tradition, or it won't be your tradition – however if you are wondering whether or not to have this, here are some things to consider.

You can create an open mike and have a few people volunteer ahead of time with a prepared talk. This allows others to feel more comfortable following, rather than being the first or only one to get up and speak. It is also helpful to give people some lead time so that they can think about what they might say. Some service leaders will announce at the beginning of the service that there will be an opportunity for people to speak later in the service. I was recently at a service for a friend that was led by the minister of her church. The minister said, "I'll give you a few minutes to think about if you want to get up and say something and for you to gather your courage!" I thought that addressed the fear factor quite nicely!

PROS

> Variety of memories
> Anyone can speak
> People feel included

CONS

> No control over content
> No control over timing

Anyone can speak (even those long-winded great uncles who just like to hear the sound of their own voices)

It may be awkward if no one takes the microphone

Projected Picture Displays

Gathering pictures of your loved one is another way of dealing with your grief. Showing the pictures to others helps both you and them to remember the good times and to say goodbye.

With the advent of digital photography, scanners, computers, projectors, PowerPoint programs and iPhoto, presenting a picture summary of a person's life projected onto the wall during the service has become much easier and popular to do. It can also be re-run at the reception afterwards. iPhoto is a program that is found on Apple Computers and is very easy to use. It is quick and easy to pop 20 pictures into it and it will give you a professional-looking presentation.

PowerPoint is a program found in PC format. It allows you to put in photographs and to add text. Personally, I like to have photographs identified. You might have heard of Aunt Edie, but you had never met her and here is a picture of her clearly identified as Aunt Eadie and Uncle Tom. Otherwise it would just be a picture of someone you didn't know.

Some programs have the capability to have music added to them as in the case of iPhoto. However others do not, or it may be more than you can accomplish. An alternative is to have someone play music while the photos are being shown. It seems to complete the presentation by having appropriate music playing.

Timing for the pictures is important. The Reverend Brian Shields, who has worked extensively with presentations of this type, recommends that you allow 6 – 8 seconds per picture. If you do not have any text, 6 seconds is enough; if you add text (and not a lot of text, just identifiers) then take 8 seconds. Once again, you have to think of the timing for the complete picture show. A good length of time is 3 minutes. This means that you can have 30 pictures in your show. (Rev. Brian Shields, personal communication, 20 March 2009)

Do a trial run. If you are putting it onto a disc or a memory stick, be sure that you have formatting that the target machine can read. Try it out at least a day ahead of time.

Include a transition slide at the beginning and at the end. This is simply a blank screen and gives the show a finished look.

Some funeral homes will create a picture presentation for you. Decide what you want before agreeing to this service.

The perfect time to show the picture presentation is after the eulogies, as this allows people time to pause and reflect on what they have heard.

Readings

These can be religious, inspirational, poetry or prose. Sometimes you will want to ask someone to read in the service. Be sure to give the person the reading ahead of time so that they can practice and be familiar with the passage. If you are asking an elderly person to read, make sure that you have increased the size of the font to 18 or 20 points on the printed word so that they can easily read it.

Music

There are many variations that you can use.

Recent surveys suggest that older people like to sing to hymns, while younger people prefer to listen to popular music and not sing along.

Live music in the form of organ or piano music with a soloist is traditional church music. You might want to have a guitar or even a band. You can have recorded music. Whatever you choose, it should be something that is reflective of the deceased – a favorite piece of their music or something that depicts their life.

I have been moved by a trumpeter at the back of the church playing "Last Call" as the final element of the service.

I was also at a memorial service for a woman of Scottish ancestry. The music as we left the church was "Amazing Grace" played on the bagpipes. Personally, I want to have "Three Times a Lady" and "Lady in Red" sung at my service.

Bev's grandchildren, aged 12 & 8, wrote and sang a song for their grandmother at her Memorial Service. The children are not musicians, but it was their way of paying tribute to their beloved grandmother. Those in attendance were heartened by the performance. At Richard's wife, Linda's service, Richard played the keyboard and a friend sang a song that Richard had written for Linda. It was tearful and memorable. Sometimes people who are close to the deceased are not a good choice for the performance as they could break down and not be able to complete their music – other times it is the icing on the cake. You will need to decide.

At the very end of a funeral of an 80-year-old community leader, Bethany, one of her friends spontaneously broke out into song. From the back of the pews, she started to sing, "You are my Sunshine." Many others joined in. It was later explained this had been Bethany's favorite song. What a wonderful way to end the service and unplanned by the family.

Broadcasting the Service to Those Unable to Attend Physically

With the advent of technology, you can now televise the funeral or memorial service anywhere in the world. Some funeral homes and religious organizations have the technology to broadcast using a webcam. If there are people who cannot attend, but would like to be there in real time, you may be able to arrange it for them providing they have a computer, the right software and connection to the internet.

Pallbearers and Casket Bearers

In many cases in our current day these are one and the same. The term *pallbearer* evolved from early Roman times when the *pallium* (or cloak) was draped over the dead body being carried to the grave. In the middle ages in Christian Europe the custom was to have a pall (a heavy rectangular cloth) covering the coffin. As the body and coffin were carried to the gravesite, some men carried the casket while others held on to cords attached to the pall so that it did not move out of place. Today, in some religious communities such as some Roman Catholic and Lutheran Churches, a large white rectangular (6x9 or 8x12 inch) piece of cloth, usually containing some decoration such as a large cross, is provided by the church to adorn the casket. In military funerals, the flag of the country is draped across the casket in place of a pall.

If you are planning to have a funeral rather than a memorial service, the funeral director will advise you to invite six (in some cases seven) strong individuals who are capable of walking a distance bearing the load. Their task will be to carry the casket from the service to the hearse after the service and then to carry it from the hearse to the gravesite at the cemetery. The funeral home may supply them with gloves for the duty.

Today pallbearers can be male or female and they can be chosen from family, close friends, co-workers or business associates, fellow members of a church or social club. When a grandparent dies, grandchildren are often invited to do this task.

The pallbearers will arrive early to the funeral to receive instructions from the funeral director. There is usually a spot in the guest book designated for the signatures of the pallbearers. They will most likely be expected to sit together in a group.

The type of clothing they wear will be up to the person planning the service. So if this is you, it will be up to you to decide whether you want the men in dark three-piece suits with a tie or if you would prefer less formality. Be sure to let them know what attire is expected when you invite them to do this task.

Honorary pallbearers are those in name only and are listed in the program as such. These may be close friends or relatives who are not able to carry a casket, or are just special people you would like to recognize.

If there is no one appropriate to be a pallbearer you can have this service included in the package from the funeral home.

The Graveside

Graveside Blessings take place when a body is being buried. There is often a car procession from the church or funeral home to the cemetery. Cars have traditionally travelled with their lights on and in quieter cities and towns other cars pull over to the side to let the procession go by. Prayers are said over the body and then the body is lowered into the grave. A symbolic spade of dirt is thrown on the coffin. In some cases, people will each have a flower to throw into the grave as a final farewell.

We are sad at funerals, but there's no such thing as a funeral without a humorous moment. Once a visiting Episcopal minister took a step backward and fell smack into the grave.

When I quoted Gayden Metcalfe back in 2009 on this page, I had no idea I would actually see this happen in front of me! Perhaps it happens more often than we would think. Be careful!

A Receiving Line

This is an important decision to make. Will the family and close friends stand and greet people? Some people may want to be a part of a receiving line while others may choose to opt out. If you decide to have one, allow your family and close friends to choose if they want to take part. People who are too young or too old may not want to participate. You may also find a way for those who are physically fragile to sit at the receiving line, or to have a chair in a place that is easy for many people to visit them.

Locate your receiving line in a place that will not obstruct entrances and exits. It could take place close to the church exit or at a spot in the reception area.

Place it in a way that allows people the choice to enter into it or not. Remember everyone grieves in a different way and some people may not be ready to talk to others. Giving people choices also allows people who don't get along or have a difficult relationship with another person to avoid having to meet face to face.

The Reception

Many people like to attend a reception afterwards in order to chat with other family members and friends. Good food and liquid refreshments are a good idea. You may have it at a hall or reception area adjacent to the service location. If you are having the service in a hall, you may just ask people to stay and circulate and bring the food in after the service is finished. Alcohol is not usually served. Some events are professionally catered, while others have food supplied by family and friends. Funeral Homes and churches often have catering and reception space available. Check with the person that you are dealing with to make these arrangements.

Often close family will assemble in someone's home after the reception; this is a more closed affair and time for family to gather together to continue the mourning and transition. If alcohol is a part of the family's life then it is appropriate to be served at this time. This after party should not take the place of a reception, however.

Things to consider:

- Who will supply the food?
- How big a space will you need?
- Do you have enough chairs?
- Who will set up and clean up?

No Service by Request

It is sad when a family does not get together because the deceased has asked them not to have a service. A basic need of human beings is to gather and celebrate and to be with each other in a time of grief. If you have a loved one who has requested "no service", I recommend that you gather your family together in some way to be together at this time. You can gather in a home, in a restaurant, at a hall, in a church, at the family summer home, on a beach, in a ski chalet. It doesn't matter where. Involve some story-telling, some food, and as many people who loved the deceased as you can. We can't turn off our emotions; we can only work through them. One of the ways that we do that is to share our stories and our feelings with others.

Examples of Programs and Other Items

When Christian's father died, the family designed a small folded-over handout with the father's picture and name of the front cover.

On the inside cover:

- His name
- Date of birth and place of birth.
- A list of family members titled "Survived by"
- "Celebration of Life"
- Date of the event
- Time
- Place
- The name of the minister
- "Cremation"

On the third page of the order of service, there was an invitation to the reception and the place it was being held.

On the back was another picture of the father with his wife. The image that was left with people was one of happiness, which is the effect that you are after.

For example:

When Thomas died of Alzheimer's disease at age 76 after a long and full life in the military, a fold-over card was handed out at his memorial service. The front and back covers held pictures of him that were taken in later life smiling and enjoying life. Inside was the story of his life. There were four pictures placed at the top and bottom of the inside pages: a baby picture, a picture of the man with his first wife, a picture of him in full military regalia and a picture of him with his second wife. The story told his life but with interesting anecdotes sprinkled throughout to make it interesting. Once again, the handout was one that brought joy to people to read and helped them to remember the good times.

Thomas Edward Brampton

Born March 28, 1929

Vancouver, British Columbia

Passed away November 20th, 2005

Victoria, British Columbia

Survived by:

Wife, *Gwynneth Marina Brampton*

Mother, *Ruth Brampton*

Father, *Fred (Shirley) Brampton*

Son, *Christian Thomas (Megan) Brampton*

Daughters, *Carol Anne (Darren) Elmquist, Terri Anne (Robert) Fry*

Sisters, *Susan Brampton, Barbara Jean (Richard) Turner, Patricia Gina (Caren Downey) Brampton*

Brothers, *Ted Jackson (Marilyn) Brampton, Bruce Brock (Tina) Brampton*

Grandchildren, *Tylor Brampton, Ricky Elmherst, Lynne Marie Fry, Anni Frampton*

Numerous nieces, nephews, and grandnieces & grandnephews

Many close friends

Celebration of Life

Saturday, November 26th, 2005

At 1:00 pm

At Saint Paul's United Church

1212 Fir Street

Vancouver, BC

Officiating: The Reverend David Greene

Cremation

Order of Service

Introduction

Music: "Because You Love Me"

Eulogy

Tributes: Ron France & Mike Millar

Scripture: Psalm 23, 1 Corinthians 13

Meditation

Prayer and Lord's Prayer

Music: "What a Wonderful World"

Blessing

"The rolling stream of life rolls on
But the recent vacant chair
Recalls the love, the smile
Of the one that once sat there."

Reception to follow the service

Friends are invited to share memories with the family in
the Banquet Room,

Saint Paul's United Church

1212 Fir Street

Vancouver BC

At any event, it is important to be clear about what is expected of the guests. An order of service or an agenda of some sort is helpful. If you cannot do that, have an usher or other hosts circulate and let people know what is happening.

The following two examples were confusing for the guests.

At Aunt Mildred's memorial service, there were tables set up with tea. People were milling about. There were tables along the side of the room with memorabilia. Jane talked to the relatives she knew and met some she hadn't seen for a while. As she had arrived about 5 minutes before the service was supposed to start, she was confused when, after 30 minutes, everyone was still milling around. Finally someone asked everyone to find a seat at a table. A man in a minister's robe stood up, introduced himself as the minister in charge, and talked about the deceased. He then asked if anyone else would like to speak. There were minutes of awkward silence and eventually three people stood up and said a few words. Then lunch was served. Jane ate lunch and continued visiting with her cousins. As people were leaving, Jane was told she was invited to the deceased woman's daughter's house. She went and had a good visit with relatives she hadn't seen for a long time. The whole day was confusing to her. She didn't know what was expected and she just went along wondering. If a program or order of service had been provided, then Jane would have felt more comfortable. Whether you have one posted on a wall or have individual ones to hand out is up to you. When people can focus on the purpose and not be wondering what is expected of them, everything will run more smoothly.

The funeral was at a golf course. The family played music on CD's that the deceased liked to listen to. No one knew what to do but to sit quietly and listen. It was just an odd time and it spoke to the fact that it was sudden, and the family did not know what to do. No one officiated and there were no stories. This was an uncomfortable situation because, once again, no direction had been given to those attending.

Chapter 3: How to Write an Obituary

What we have done for ourselves alone
dies with us; what we have done for others
and the world remains and is immortal.
Albert Pike

What is an Obituary?

The Merriam-Webster dictionary defines *obituary* as a notice of a person's death usually with a short biographical account.

Obituary notices can be found in most local newspapers and now online at Obituary Websites.

Although some people write their own obituary to be ready for publication upon their death, usually a close family member will write the notice.

The purpose of an obituary is not only to announce a person's death to the community but also to let friends, family and business acquaintances know when, and if, there will be a funeral or memorial service and to give the details.

The Purpose of an Obituary

An obituary is about a life lived as opposed to a death that has occurred; it is the public notice that goes out into the newspaper and is seen by the population at large. Certainly you are letting people know that death has happened, but the majority of your article should be to celebrate the life of your loved one. In this short space you want to quickly and succinctly give the readers a clear and concise snapshot of the life of someone they may have loved. It may be their first knowledge of the death.

How to Write an Obituary

Writing the obituary is the prelude to writing and presenting the eulogy. You want to be accurate, interesting and full of little details that make up the dash between the years of birth and death.

The following will give you options to choose from when you are writing an obituary. Pick and choose the appropriate information in telling the story of the deceased's life.

Where Should You Post an Obituary?

1. The local newspaper.

2. The local newspaper of the family living in other areas of the country or world.

3. The local newspaper in the town where the person spent much of their life and still has family or friends residing.

4. Internet Memorial Sites such as: InMemoriam.ca; Memories.net; Legacy.com; Remembered.com.

If you are placing the obituary in a newspaper or online, you can refer to the other listings to give you ideas. Newspapers often refer people to an online guestbook and you may want to go and leave your condolences and comments in the guestbook. You can also upload pictures to the site.

Components of an Obituary with Examples and Comments

Name/Announcement of the birth and death. Include maiden names and other married names if appropriate to make it easier for friends to identify the individual.

Name commonly used. Include the name the person went by (i.e. nickname). Leave out the middle name unless it is important to identify the person. *Thomas (Tom) Frederick Tulk* can simply be listed as *Thomas (Tom) Tulk,* but *John Thomas Smith* may be needed to let people know which John Smith has died. *Priscilla (Cilla) Lidstone Nee Green. Nee* means born and therefore is used to denote a maiden name.

Year of birth and date of death. You may choose to state how old the person is; however, it is not necessary and is sometimes seen as redundant. Be careful of how much information you put into the newspaper because identity theft can happen. *Born 1938 – Died March 5, 2009*, or *Died March 5, 2009 at the age of 81 years*, or *81 years old.*

Place of birth and death. *Born in St. John's, Newfoundland and died in Victoria, British Columbia.*

Cause of death. Use only if appropriate: Died in a fatal car accident, Died after a lengthy battle with cancer, Peacefully in her sleep, Suddenly, Tragically.

Predeceased by Include parents, spouse, siblings, children. *Predeceased by his parents and his beautiful daughter, Margaret.*

Remembered by or survived by: Usually close relatives are included, but you may add any other special friends that the deceased may have wanted named. Spouse/partner, children, grandchildren, great grandchildren, parents, grandparents, siblings. Others such as nephews, nieces, cousins, in-laws, friends, or pets. It is important to identify the relationship and not just list the names.

Children, grandchildren, etc., should be in order of date of birth.

Spouses of the person's children go in brackets immediately following the child's name. Any grandchildren can be listed all together in the next sentence.

John is survived by his wife of 57 years, Della, and his three sons and their families: Thomas (Cindy), Richard

(Janice) and James (Gerald); and by his six grandchildren, Tyler, Ben, Michael, Paige, Sheryl, and Charles.

Although some people add pets' names, I would suggest that you do this only in special circumstances, such as a pet that stayed on the bed with the deceased throughout her palliative care.

Life of the Deceased: You can include any of the following: Childhood, family life, schools, friends, education, degrees received, designations, awards, other recognition, employment, projects, activities, qualities, places of residence, hobbies & interests, affiliations, achievements, unusual attributes, humor, or other stories.

Born in County Cork, the third son in a family of 12. John left school in the 8th grade to help support his family. He immigrated to Canada when he was 18 and took a job working on the docks on the West Coast. He eventually started his own contracting company, which one of his sons continues to run to this day. Although John did not complete high school as a boy, he returned to his studies in his 50's and received an MBA at the age of 60 years, graduating at the same time as his son Jimmy.

In 1952, John married Della and they raised four children: Thomas, Richard, Margaret and James. A committed family man, John coached soccer throughout the boys' time in school. John won "Father of the Year Award" in 1973.

41

The Service. Be sure to give all the needed and relevant information: Day, date, time, place; Name of officiant, Visitation information if applicable: day, date, time, place; Reception information if applicable: day, date, time, place; Other memorial, vigil, or graveside services if applicable: day, date, time, place. Place of internment; Name of funeral home in charge of arrangements and, in some cases, a phone number; Where to call for more information (even if no service is planned). Any other details, such as officiant, pallbearers, etc., can be learned at the service.

A memorial service will be held at St. Julian's-by-the-Sea, 1285 Seaside Place at 10:00 a.m. Wednesday, June 15.

Visitations will take place at the Peacock Funeral Home Thursday and Friday, August 22nd and 23rd, between 2 and 3 p.m. The funeral will be held at 3:00 p.m. on Friday, August 23rd.

If the reception is a different day, different time or different location from the Memorial Service and you think there will be people who may want to attend one and not the other, then I suggest you include this in the obituary. Although some funeral/memorial guides suggest a phone number to call, my suggestion is that it isn't needed. Use it only if you can see a specific need.

End the obituary on a positive note: Memorial funds established; Memorial donation suggestions, including addresses; Thank you to people, groups or institutions. In this section you may want to thank people who have helped your loved one at the end of their life and who most likely won't be attending their funeral. This could be nursing staff, palliative care staff, paramedics, etc.

Donations to the (name of fund) *would be appreciated.* Or: *Please donate to the charity of your choice in memory of* (name).

Many people like to be able to donate in memory of the deceased. This has replaced the once common tradition of sending flowers. For many years the words "In lieu of flowers" were commonly used. As the custom is now more prevalent to send to a charity, it is acceptable to omit the phrase.

If the charity sends a list of names to you to let them know who has donated in the name of your loved one, you can send them a thank you note.

A special thank you to the staff of 4 West who took such cheerful care of Lottie in her last days.

A note about the word, die. How do you say "die"? You might want to use any of these: Passed away; deceased; passed on; moved on; crossed the vale; crossed over; gone; departed; gone home; gone to the great (favorite place/activity) in the sky; bid farewell; lost his/her life.

Obituary Photographs

A complementary picture of the person is helpful to the reader. Some people also choose to have a younger and an older picture in the paper and this is equally acceptable.

The question of what picture, if any, should you include in the obituary is one that is often asked. Funeral directors and clergy suggest that you think about which picture will most celebrate the life of the deceased. The picture should be one that shows the personality or enhances the memory of the person. You can have a current picture (interestingly enough, one that could have been taken within the last 15 years, according to social-work professor, Keith Anderson of Ohio State University) or a picture that was taken at a highlight in the person's life. My mother loved being in the navy. There were some great snapshots of her in full uniform. That would have been very appropriate even though these photos were taken in her early 30's and she died at 81. Mary loved her little dog and in later life it was what kept her laughing. Her family chose to put a two-year-old picture of the 85-year-old into the paper with the dog on her lap. Fred was the most wonderful grandfather and his family chose to place a picture in the obituary column with him and his two young grandchildren perched on his knee. Thomas was standing behind the wheel of his yacht. The picture was approximately 10 years old. My friend Mary Anne died in her 50's. The picture that her husband chose for the obituary was Mary Anne in the dress she had made as mother of the groom at her son's wedding, which took place 2 years before she died. She was smiling with joy and pride of her son in the picture. Very appropriate.

Some people choose to add a quote, a poem, or even a few words to sum up the person's life.

There are many quote sites on the internet from which you can put in a keyword that is appropriate for your story and come up with suitable quotes.

Examples:

We are not human beings having a spiritual experience. We are spiritual beings having a human experience. Teilhard de Chardin (1881-1955)

If I could wish for my life to be perfect, it would be tempting but I would have to decline, for life would no longer teach me anything. Allyson Jones

We are shaped and fashioned by what we love. Johann Wolfgang von Goethe (1749-1832)

Life is just a chance to grow a soul. A. Powell Davies (1902-1957)

And in the end, it's not the years in your life that count. It's the life in your years. Abraham Lincoln (1809-1865)

For death is no more than a turning of us over from time to eternity. William Penn (1644-1718)

Is death the last sleep? NO – it is the last and final awakening. Sir Walter Scott (1771-1832)

Because I have loved life, I shall have no sorrow to die.
Amelia Burr (1878-1968)

People living deeply have no fear of death. Anais Nin
(1903-1977)

Let us be kinder to one another. Aldous Huxley (1894-
1963)

A woman asked her local newspaper editor to publish a
long, detailed obituary about her husband, one she had
written herself. But when she learned the cost would be 50
cents a word, she said, "Well, just say 'Jack Smith died.'"
But there's a seven-word minimum, ma'am, the editor said
politely. "OK," she said, "just say 'Jack Smith died; 2004
pick-up for sale.'"

Tips:

- Check with your local newspaper to find out the
  publication deadline, cost and any rules and
  restrictions they may have for an obituary listing.

- Most newspapers charge by the word or by the line to
  publish obituaries. Keep it brief if money is an issue.

- Read other obituaries in your local newspaper to
  understand the style and to get ideas.

- Don't be afraid to ask for ideas and stories from
  friends and family.

- Write in the third person (for example: don't say 'Mom' or 'I'). Remember the obituary is about the deceased, not about you or your relationship to that person.

- When listing family members, decide how many you want to include. If you include one grandparent, then include all the grandparents. If you include the name of one grandchild, then include the names of all the grandchildren. Don't forget step-family members.

- Give a little story of the person's life.

- Don't use just words to describe the person – tell stories to describe how the person "gave his time and money to help the cause of the abandoned cats in our city" instead of "charitable person".

- Write in a logical flow.

- Add an interesting bit of information that will make the reader feel good and will present the deceased in a good light.

- Honor the memory of the person you are writing about and leave out any negative comments or stories.

- Check the spelling of all names and the accuracy of the dates. Did you put the numbers in the right order?

- Have others read it and give you feedback about the flow and whether there have been any errors or omissions. What you might not see, someone else might.

- Any writing project consists of writing it, then rewriting it, until you get it right. Don't be afraid to cross out and start again or add to your first draft.

- Proofread – more than once!

- Write the article one day and set aside. Re-read it the next day and correct any errors or omissions that you may have made.

- If you do make a mistake in the paper, contact them immediately and correct the error for the next publication date. If on the internet, republish.

- Once the obituary is published, keep several copies for relatives and friends who live out of town, and for family that does genealogy or other family memory work. Forward the website to family and friends.

- Take proper precautions to safeguard the identity of the deceased before posting the obituary in the newspaper, on the web or anywhere else.

Things to Avoid and Common Mistakes:

- Using clichés

- Negativity

- Starting with "the family regrets to announce"

- Writing a eulogy and using it as an obituary

- Writing a page-length column

- Incomplete or inaccurate list of family members

- Misspelling

- Writing a dull listing without interesting facts (i.e. she was the mayor of the town for 15 years; he was 100 years old)

- Jumping all over with your facts

- Including the details of the friends and family that could be used instead in the eulogy

- Forgetting to check or have someone check your spelling and your grammar

- Rambling

- Being long-winded

Due to identity fraud, do not give date of birth details, middle name or initial, or home address.

How to Credit an Ex-Spouse

Warren's parents were divorced but on friendly terms. His father died. Warren felt he could not put his mother's name under the surviving relatives, but he wanted to give mention to the woman who had been his father's wife and business partner for 25 years. In telling the story of his father's business, he mentioned his mother by name giving her full credit as a substantial part of his father's life.

Mixed Messages

One family wrote "With mixed emotions, we announce the peaceful passing of our mother." The immediate question that springs to the reader's mind is "What kind of mixed emotions? Didn't they like her?" The family may have been happy that the mother was no longer suffering from old age or chronic diseases, but it does leave a question in the readers' minds that should not be there. It is always best to tell the story in the third person to eliminate any of these kinds of mistakes.

Preventing Identity Theft

Identity Theft is a real problem these days and growing. It is important to leave out certain details that will help thieves use the information of the deceased. Don't use the full name of the deceased. Don't use the full date of birth – year only is better. The following checklist of things to do before you post the obituary in the paper or a Memorial site will help to stop the would-be thieves from using any information to get credit or false identification. Why bother? Besides the obvious moral issues of the matter, thieves can cause problems to surviving relatives by tying up joint credit accounts and stealing existing cash in bank accounts.

Checklist: Important actions to take to stop thieves from stealing the deceased's identity

Experts recommend that you notify all agencies and businesses that were used by the deceased by telephone and follow up with a written letter and copy of the death certificate. These actions should be taken before posting the obituary and before the notice of the funeral goes out. Check with your lawyer or other professional for actions to take in your locality. Here is a guideline to get you started.

1. Notify the credit reporting agencies in your area and ask them to place a "Deceased Alert" on the credit report. You may also want to request a copy of the credit report to make sure no illegal activity has happened (this may especially be true if the deceased has been ill or incapacitated for any length of time before the death).

2. Notify all the deceased's creditors such as credit card companies, mortgage and loan holders. Even though you have alerted the Credit Reporting Agency, not all creditors will check with them before issuing a new account to an existing customer. Ask them to list it as "Closed. Account holder is deceased."

3. Cancel the deceased's Social Insurance Number. (In some countries babies are issued with social security numbers or social insurance numbers and so it is

important to do this regardless of the age of the deceased.)

4. Obtain at least 12 copies of the death certificate, which is supplied to the Funeral Home from the coroner.

5. Notify the deceased's financial advisor.

6. For joint accounts with spouse (or other person) remove the name from the account or close the account and reopen in the remaining spouse's name.

7. Also notify:

- Auto, health, life insurance companies
- Veteran's administration agency if the person was in your country's military
- Immigration Service if the deceased immigrated to their current country
- Government department responsible for the deceased's driving license
- Any professional organizations the deceased belonged to – bar associations, medical licensing agency, Association of Professional Engineering, etc.
- Any membership programs such as the public library, fitness clubs, etc.

The Identity Theft Resource Centre recommends that you include the following information on all letters:

- Name and social security number or social insurance number of the deceased;
- Last known addresses for the previous 5 years;
- Date of birth and death;
  - All requested documentation specific to that agency in the first letter to speed up processing.
- Send all by mail which requires a signature upon receipt.
- Keep copies of all correspondence, noting date sent and any response(s) you receive.

Sample Obituaries

Some Good Examples

JAMES, Alexander

Passed away peacefully, with his family at his side May 24th, 2009 at the age of 85.

Alex was born in Yorkshire, England where he attended school at St. Stephen's College. He was an avid sportsman joining the rugby, lacrosse and football teams. From 1939-45, he had a very distinguished military career, serving with the Royal Artillery as a Lance Bombardier. In 1940, he went to France and was evacuated from Dunkirk, crossing the channel in a trawler. Later, as a Captain with the 662 Air O.P. Squadron, he piloted Auster aircraft and was present at the Normandy invasion on D-day in 1944 and received the Distinguished Flying Cross later that same year. After the war, he continued in service, rejoining the Territorial Army in 1947 and the Royal Auxiliary Air Force in 1950 as Commander of an Air O.P. Flight at Hendon. Alex immigrated to Canada in 1953 and joined Imperial Oil Ltd. In 1967 he became Computer Operations Manager for the Alberta Dept. of Education and later, Manager, Computer Services for the Edmonton Board of Education. He retired in 1985 to Victoria.

He is survived by his loving wife of 55 years, Sharon, and his children, Tony (Sandra), Jack (Barbara), Brenda (Larry), Jeff (Carol); his grandchildren, Bob, Tyler, Stephen, Casey and Brady, and his sister Theresa (Fred) Simmons in England.

The family wishes to thank Dr. Hagen with the deepest gratitude, along with the staff at Elderberry Hospital for the compassion and dignity provided to Dad under their care.

Donations may be made to the B.C. Aviation Museum in Sidney B.C.

Alex requested no formal service but would like his family and friends to gather in his honor at the B.C. Aviation Museum on Friday, June 4th, 2009 from 2-5p.m. All are welcome.

MOFFAT, Joan (nee Burton) Passed away peacefully on June 15, 2008 in Sydney, Australia at the age of 91 years young.

She was born in Sussex, England. She was predeceased by her brother Scott of Somerset, England in 1988 and she is survived by her husband of 65 years, Frederick, her brother Tom, of Paris, France, her son Christian (Marlene) of New Orleans, Louisiana, her daughter Hilary Perry (Gordon) of Bainbridge Island, Washington, six grandchildren, and three great grandchildren. Joan's father served in the Royal Air Force for many years and the family lived at several stations in England as well as in India and Egypt. She also spent two years in Singapore and one year in Hong Kong with family friends in the late 1930s. Early in WWII, Joan joined the Women's Auxiliary of the Royal Air Force (W.A.A.F.), became a Codes and Cyphers Officer, and served at several stations including Oban, Scotland where she met her husband to be, Frederick. They were married in Edinburgh in December 1943 and moved to Canada late in the war. The following 22 years of Canadian Air Force life included stops in Vancouver, Ottawa, Toronto, Halifax, Greenwood, Norfolk (USA) and Prince Edward Island. This was followed by retirement to Sydney, Australia in 1966 – a place they had always dreamed of living. Joan was an accomplished cook, athlete (golfing, curling), watercolor artist and amateur actress, and she thoroughly enjoyed life.

There will be no service, by request, but following cremation there will be an informal gathering of family and friends.

xxx

Robert E. Lidstone

Robert E. Lidstone, CPA, 56, of Wenatchee died Wednesday, April 15, 2009.

Services will be at 10 a.m. Monday in Hillside Christian Church with the Rev. Roy T. Trainer and the Rev. Linus Carter officiating. Private family burial will be in Memorial Park Cemetery by Superior Funeral Home, 1980 Crest Drive.

Robert Edward Lidstone was born in 1952, to John M. Lidstone and Nancy Powell Lidstone. He grew up in Wenatchee and graduated from Crest High School with the class of 1969. He served his country in the Navy and graduated with his bachelor's in accounting from Washington State University. Robert married Mary Lynn Myers in 1981 and raised her two daughters, Michelle Susan and Tanya Sara, as his own. He and Mary had two sons, John Edward and Jacob Ryan. They raised their four children in Wenatchee. During this time, Robert built up Lidstone and Associates as a successful CPA firm.

Robert was a wonderful and devoted father, as well as a great friend. He was also a loving "Papa" to his eight grandchildren. Robert was a very honest and giving man. He had a big heart and loved everyone. Robert was blessed with great friends, a wonderful family and great success. His favorite saying was "Life is good."

He was preceded in death by two brothers, Brian Lidstone in 1979 and Bruce Lidstone in 2004.

John's request was that memorials be to Wenatchee Children's Research Hospital, 1501 Thompson Place, Wenatchee; or Special Children's Fund, 8888 Emery Parkway, Walla Walla.

The family will receive friends from 6 to 8 p.m. Sunday at the funeral home.

xxx

MILLER, Ronald - P.Eng. 1924 – 2009 Queen's Science '47 (Engineering)

Ron was born in New York City, and passed away at home in Toronto, surrounded by his loved ones. Ron is survived by Gwen, his beloved wife of 56 years. Loving father of Maggie Ryerson (Tim Jones) of Toronto, Caroline Joan of New York, Pamela (Roger Harris) of Perth and Peter of Toronto. Proud Grandfather of Jen (Andrew), Kate, Ben, Larissa, Isaac, Heather Lynn (Jonathan), Reba, Daniel and James. Ron is survived by his sister, Beverly Holden, and predeceased by his sister Joanne Markenham, and brothers Will, Bob, Jack (Jean), Norm (Jenny) and Bert (Pat Keene).

He will be missed by many nieces and nephews. In Ron's career with the Government of Canada, he worked on the Canso Causeway, the St. Lawrence Seaway, was Chief of Canals and Assistant Director of Forestry Canada, Ontario region. After retirement he spent some years working in real estate, travel and Ontario Electric. He volunteered with the Cancer Society, the Toronto South Community Association and was an active member of several service organizations. Ron was well known for his sense of humor, his love of family, his ability to fix absolutely anything, and his joy in friendship.

Special thanks to Dr. Terrance Shields for his many years of excellent care and to Ron's wonderful caregivers: Karen, Kathy, and Bart.

At Ron's request there will be no visitation. The family will receive friends at St. Andrew's Presbyterian Church, 1225 Barnhill Road, after 1p.m. on April 27th, 2009 until time of service in the church at 2 p.m. Reception will follow in the church hall. Donations to the Cancer Society Foundation would be appreciated. Funeral arrangements entrusted to the Canada Chapel of Special Souls.

Hard to Write

Daniel Elisha Rodders, infant son of Dr. John and Susanne (Tipping) Rodders, entered the kingdom of heaven on Feb. 7, 2008. In addition to his parents, Daniel will be deeply missed by his maternal grandparents, Darlene and Michael Tipping, Edward Candace Campbell; paternal grandparents, Dale and Lynne Lindsey; Jerry and Lara Rodders; great-grandmothers, Janet King; Ann Rodders; paternal great-grandfather, Malcolm Bennett; Aunt Sheri Gates; Uncle John and Aunt Debbie Rodders; aunt Julia Rodders; and cousins, Brittany and Ben Gates and Nicholas Rodders.

Seeing your face was truly seeing an angel. To hold you in our arms was a gift of everlasting love. Your tiny feet made footprints forever on our hearts. When the sun and stars shine brightly or as the rains fall, we'll think of you, smiling down on us. Until we meet again.

Private funeral services will be held on Monday, Feb. 16, 2008 in the Everlasting Funeral Home & Cremation Service, 1445 Market St., Newark, with the Rev. Richard Bloom, pastor of the Newark United Methodist Church officiating.

RUSSELL, Charles (Chas) Timothy ended his life in the afternoon, April 11, 2009, at his London home.

Survived and deeply loved by his mother Anna and his sister Cynthia with husband Tom and nephew Christoff. Predeceased by his father Jackson in 1979. Grieved by family and friends everywhere, mainly in England and Canada.

Chas was born in London in 1965, raised at the family ranch in Alberta Canada., and then in Banff and Penticton, B.C. He graduated in 1983 from Penticton Secondary School, graduated with a B.Sc. Biology (First Class) from UBC in 1987, and attended two years at the UBC Faculty of Medicine, before discovering he really wanted to study architecture. In 1995 Chas received his M.Arch. from the UBC School of Architecture and then enjoyed work in London England, including opening his own office in late 2007.

Chas was kind, faithful, generous, gentle, intelligent, caring and compassionate. He loved nature, hiking, skiing and paddling, and his guitars. He was always there for anyone in need and had so much insight into what troubled him. Until the very end, Chas kept searching for some lightness of being. Why did you leave so soon?

Come gather to remember Chas, Saturday, April 25, 2009, 2-5 p.m. at Victoria House, 18 Piccadilly Circus, London.

A fund in Chas' name has been set up at the Beautiful Skies Conservation Council of England, phone 555-555-5787, bscc@beautifulskiesconservationcouncil.org.

In one of the stars, I shall be living. In one of them, I shall be laughing. And so it will be as if all the stars were laughing when you look at the sky at night.

A Really Bad Example of an Obituary:

I chose this one out of a local newspaper because it jumped around and confused the reader (I changed the identifying names and activities). If you don't know how to write – put down your thoughts and have another person read it and help you put it into order. I have only included a part of this very lengthy obit. It was actually a newspaper page long!

> Wilma Smith. Wilma's first name is Susan but her parents called her Wilma from the day of her birth. Wilma grew up on in what was the small town on the banks of the Rambling River – Littleton, AD. Her father and grandfather owned and operated a hardware store called Bakerson's Hardware. Wilma worked in the store in the 1950's and 1960's. Wilma died suddenly which was a shock to her family and her many friends. She died May 10th, 2009 at 7:03 p.m. from complications from elective surgery. Wilma was born in Bigtown on November 12, 1941. She was a young 67-year-old when she died. She returned to live

here after 10 years living in the East in 1977. Because both she and her husband (Tom Smith) of 45 years are only children, Wilma was concerned that she was depriving their grandparents of the chance to spoil her children. She was predeceased by her parents Elsie and Edward. Wilma was an avid seamstress and in recent years had turned to quilting and has created some magnificent creations that adorn the walls of her house. She worked for years at Hemlines on Main Street. She has been a member of the Main Street Quilt Guild and her husband has spent many hours reading books, which he enjoys, outside of quilt stores and fabric stores all across North America. She has two lovely and accomplished children Tim the first born and Pauline the baby. Pauline's husband is in the Navy and is on deployment in his navy ship, the Don Perkins. She has four grandchildren that she adores and as grandma's do spoils them with gifts and loving tender care. Billy was her first grandchild and the second grandchild is Tony and the third grandchild is Taylor and to round out the list Bobby is the fourth grandchild. They are all special to Wilma in their own different ways. She loved them dearly and had a very special place in her heart for each of them. Donna Smith, her son's ex-wife remains a member of the family in Wilma's view of the world. She has some amazing friends as well, her long-time buddy and one-time boss is Ruth O'Malley who was once the owner of Hemlines they talked daily and often twice daily.

There was a raucous bunch of women Wilma played golf with included in the list are Mary, Donna, Janet, and sometimes fill-ins for these busy women Candace, Shelly, and Clarice. Your last names have been omitted to protect the innocent. Other friends from her days in the East are Gerry and Linda Campbell who Bill biked with for two weeks in France and then the ladies met up with them at the end of the trip and the explored Paris. Joan and Ken have been close friends since arriving in this city in 1977. They met when their sons were signing up for football. Over the years a friendship developed between the families and there have been many adventures that they enjoyed together.

Chapter 4: How to Write a Eulogy

*They say such nice things about people at
their funerals that it makes me sad that
I'm go to miss mine by just a few days.*
Garrison Kiellor

What is a Eulogy?

The Merriam-Webster dictionary defines *eulogy* as a
speech given in tribute, especially one praising someone
who has died.

In early Greek times, approximately 2,500 years ago, men
who were killed in war were given elaborate tributes
praising the deeds that they did for their country. Today a
eulogy is a snapshot of a life, looked at through positive
lenses, to celebrate and remember the loved one who has
just died. A eulogy can be a story of the deceased's life in
chronological order or it can be a group of stories from the
eulogist's point of view and relationship with the
deceased.

Introduction

Writing the eulogy can be therapeutic and healing not only
for you, but for those in the audience. Some people prefer
to have a minister or funeral director eulogize their loved
one. Others prefer to speak. Sometimes people think they
don't want to give the eulogy and then change their mind.
If that is the case for you, go for it. Don't be afraid to tell

the minister or the funeral director that you now want to be the one to give the tribute. If you keep quiet, you may regret that decision later.

If you do not want to write and present the eulogy yourself, you can also write the eulogy and ask someone else to read it for you. When my ex-husband died, my son really wanted to do the eulogy for his father but he was having a hard time getting started. I wrote page one and he wrote page two. No one ever knew that he hadn't done the whole thing (until now!).

One of the biggest honors I have felt occurred when I was able to eulogize the person I love. Actually I have written two eulogies in my life that have touched my soul. One was the eulogy I presented for my mother and the other was the one I helped my son write for his father.

You have only a few short days to put together this eulogy – unless you are preparing ahead of time, which is also a good idea. I have put together the steps for you to take that will help you create the eulogy that will bring you pride and honor for the person you are eulogizing.

Length of a Eulogy

Always check with the funeral director or minister who is arranging the service to find out what they have planned in the way of timing. If only one person is giving the eulogy, the eulogy could be fifteen minutes however if there are more than one speaker it is usually best to keep the length to five to seven minutes per person.

You can plan on one minute per one hundred words as a rough guide. Most word processors have a function called *word count*, which saves you from counting each word yourself.

Types of Eulogies

The format of the eulogy you write will depend on your style: the type of person you are; the type of presentation you feel comfortable delivering, and how your tribute fits into the service as a whole.

Two types:

1. Short Biography
2. Collection of stories about the person

Ideas for Eulogies

1. When you are writing a historical, chronological story of the person's life (short biography), choose aspects from the list below:

   - The name of the person who passed away

   - When he/she was born

   - When he/she died

   - Who he/she was to you: friend, relative, etc.

- Stories from her/his childhood

- Education received

- Career highlights

- Marriage(s)

- Children/grandchildren

- Special interests or hobbies

- Obstacles they encountered and triumphed over

- Retirement

- Crowning glories

- Three words to summarize this person

- A final goodbye

2. When you are writing a eulogy consisting of a collection of stories about the person, choose aspects from the list below: (These will be stories from your experience, or that you have found or heard, that go together to give a picture of what the person was like.)

- The name of the person who passed away

- When he/she was born

- When he/she died

- Who he/she was to you: friend, relative, etc.

- Why this person mattered to you

- Stories that only the two of you experienced together

- How he/she changed your world and/or the world around you

- Why you'll always remember the person

- A final goodbye

Other questions that can help you write a eulogy:

1. What was this person's personality like?

2. How long have you known the person?

3. How did you meet?

4. What was this person's life like growing up?

Rachel Marie Hall was born on a farm in the middle of the prairie on March 3, 1934. She grew up in a faithful Presbyterian family with 3 older brothers and one younger sister.

5. What aspect of the person did you treasure the most?

6. What memory stands out when you think of this person?

When I think of Rachel, I think of a person who had so much energy and excitement for life. When I was first learning to golf, Rachel, Yvonne and I would golf every morning over the school summer holidays. One morning on the 4th hole, I sunk the ball on my second shot. I was amazed, and I stood there dumbfounded. But not Rachel. She started shrieking and jumping up and down. She caused so much noise, players on the other fairways came to see what was happening. It was my shot, but it was her excitement! I made her day! I bet many others of you have had a similar experience when spending time with Rachel.

7.   What are some of his/her greatest accomplishments? Personal, Spiritual, Career.

Speaking of Rachel, I'm not sure if her flying career, her music career, her teaching career or her being a mother was her greatest achievement, but I know that she squeezed every ounce of juice out of each moment of her life. She was devoted to her church community. Once she moved to the Island she became fanatical about garage sales and I remember arriving for a visit one day to view her latest purchases filling up the dining room table. Her husband, Jim, was saying "Rachel, you have to stop this – we're running out of room and we can't afford a bigger house!"

8.   Was there a time when she/he showed great courage, conviction, or another attribute?

Rachel wasn't afraid to be a 40-year-old student at college while most of the other students in the class were in their early 20's. She wanted to get a teaching degree and she did!

9. Was there a lesson that you learned from this person that you can share with others?

Rachel went back to university when she was 40-years-old. She became an elementary school teacher and loved her job. It was Rachel who encouraged me to go back and get a degree. I have always been thankful to her for being a role model. It changed my life!

Some people suggest that you think of three words that sum up the person's life and use them to help you write your eulogy. You can use them in this manner:

When I think of Rachel three words come to mind: energetic, exciting, inspiring. I'd like to tell you a story that demonstrates these three words.... Rachel liked to be the center of attention and she went to great lengths to make sure that she made a positive impression. She practiced and practiced a few lively songs on the piano, including Boogey Woogey Bugle Boy of Company B. Whenever she was at a public event that had a piano in the room, she would sit down at the piano and play a couple of these lively songs. She told me that she loved getting the compliments afterwards.

Technology Can Help:

There are many ways to deliver a eulogy. Shawn is up on technology. He creates websites and he communicates with everyone using his cell phone to send and receive email and to keep up with what his friends are doing on Facebook and Twitter. Shawn told me this story:

When my young cousin was in hospital last November, I went to see her every day, talked to her doctors and nurses, then went on my cellphone to email the family updates.

When she died at the end of November, a simple ceremony was held at the cemetery in Chilliwack. After the priest finished and her two brothers spoke, it was my turn to give a eulogy. I used my phone to refer to the notes and conversations we had.

Afterwards my cousin told me it was so appropriate that I read from my phone because it was so key in keeping them informed of their sister. (Shawn O'Hara, email communication, May 29, 2009)

Ideas that can be entertaining and creative:

- A song and dance number
- A comedic sketch
- A mini-play
- A short film or slide show
- A documentary

72

- A poem
- An *elegy* – a long poem written to pay tribute to the departed
- A short story

Step-by-Step Process to Create a Eulogy

Step 1: Take Time to Contemplate

Make friends with the angels, who though invisible are always with you…Often invoke them, constantly praise them, and make good use of their help and assistance in all your temporal and spiritual affairs. St. Francis de Sales (1567-1622)

Take time to contemplate. Some people journal. Some people go for a walk. Some people sit down with a cup of tea or other liquid and chat with friends about their dear departed loved one. Do whatever it is that helps you to ground yourself.

Don't worry if you cry during this time. It is natural to be emotional. For some people, the expression of feelings comes easily; for other people it comes from a much deeper and foreign place. It is natural and healthy to cry, to feel disoriented, to want to deny what has happened, to feel angry. You will go through many of these emotions. Take some time to feel what you are experiencing and to gather the strength that you will need to get through these next few hours and days as you do the very public part of your grieving.

As you prepare to write and deliver a eulogy for your loved one, remember that no one has ever delivered the perfect eulogy. Remember that there may be tears and crying even as you deliver the eulogy.

At this step, I suggest that you find a quiet space (outdoors or indoors) and think about the person you knew and loved.

Imagine the person's face in your mind. Go back to a time when they were healthy and happy and the two of you were spending time together. See the love in their eyes, hear the laughter and enjoy the moment that you shared together. Hold that image as a lasting memory.

Picture the face of the person, remember the sound of their voice, feel the touch of their body, recall the stories they used to enjoy telling, recollect their favorite activities.

The following exercise will help you invoke your memories.

Find a comfortable, quiet spot where you won't be disturbed. Read through this exercise once and then go back and read it slowly, following the instructions as you go. If you prefer you can read it onto a tape slowly and then play it back. Either way will work.

Sit in a comfortable position with your feet flat on the floor and your arms resting comfortably at your sides.

Close your eyes. Breathe deeply three times. As you inhale, count to 10, feel the healing, life-giving air surging into your entire body. Hold that breath for 10 seconds. As you exhale, count to 10.

As you are counting, visualize any impurities, hurts or negative thoughts leaving your body.

Think back to a happy memory with your loved one who has just passed away.

Remember them in a healthy time. Picture that person in your mind...

Notice their features... notice the clothing they were wearing... hear their voice or perhaps their laughter...

Listen to anything that your loved one had said to you at that time...- - - take as many minutes as you need for these memories - - -

What would your loved one want you to say about them in your eulogy? Make a mental list.

Remember laughter... remember challenges...remember achievements...remember the normal and everyday parts of that person's life...

Remember your relationship and gather inner strength from its joy..

Take time to think about some of the good times you shared together.

Think of any of the stories that this person told you about in their life.

Think of any funny events that you shared together.

Take time. Sit and remember.

Be still and remember your loved one.

When you are ready to end this session, do so by taking three more deep, slow breaths and when you are ready, slowly open your eyes and re-enter the present moment in the place where you are at.

Step 2: Gather Your Stories

- Now take a pen and paper or computer keyboard and jot down any ideas that have formed during this time. It may be in the form of a list or in the form of stories or even bits of stories. This will be the beginning of your eulogy preparation. Make notes of your own memories.

- Talk to family and friends and note memories that they suggest. Remember to ask the children as well as the adults.

- Jot down other stories that people have told you about this person.

- Look at written documents, memorabilia and picture albums left behind by the deceased.

- Create a timeline of events. Don't be too concerned about the exact dates – be general.

- Various family members may remember events in different ways. When creating your presentation, use words and phrases that allow each person to understand the story in their own way. For example, your sister might remember that your mother starred in her first musical production in 1950. You are sure that it was in 1954. Instead of using a year, talk about the excitement when, as a young woman, your mother first starred in a musical number and how she continued to partake in this kind of activity until she was in her late 70's. Another example is that you may have found that your uncle was a very caring person while other family members lived in fear of him. You can make a statement such as: *Family members saw Uncle Fred in different ways. My experience was that he always had a kind word and a bag full of candy for me when I visited.* In this way you are acknowledging others' experience while being true to your own experience.

- Jot down as many points as you think of – you can eliminate the ones you don't want later.

- Think about what the person meant to you and write down some words.

- Think about some of the memorable times you had together and make a note of some points that will remind you.

- Think of some of the quiet day-to-day times that you had together. Jot down a description in point form. Each weeknight we would set the coffee pot to come on in the morning so that when we woke up we would literally smell the coffee. Our daily routine was to get up, have coffee and toast together and map out our days. We would discuss the events and when we would see each other again. My mother was a busy person in her volunteer work and I was always pleased to know that we would have that morning time together. Tom and I will miss our mornings with Mom!

- Add a list of stories that the person used to tell about themselves and their experiences, or stories they wrote about in their memoirs.

- List the qualities of this person.

- List any favorite poems or stories that they may have written, enjoyed reading, or that seem appropriate.

Once you have all this material, decide which of these items you will want to use in your tribute to your loved one. You will not want to use all of them (think of less than 10 minutes worth of material). Be sure to include stories that will bring a smile to your face.

Step 3: Craft Your Speech

A speech should always have an opening, body and closing. You tell them what you are going to tell them, you tell them, and you tell them what you told them.

By now you will have decided if you are going to present a brief history or a collection of stories.

Here are some general rules that will help you write a great eulogy:

- Introduce yourself and state your relationship with the deceased
- Talk about what you know
- Remember that the focal point of the eulogy is the person who died, not you.
- Start and end strongly
- Start with the big picture
- Put your stories and comments together into a logical or chronological order
- Use the number *three*:
  - 3 main points
  - 3 characteristics you want to highlight
  - 3 stories
  - 3 areas of the deceased's life, i.e. growing up/family/career OR early life/work life/later years

- Be descriptive. Instead of "Aunt Amy wore provocative clothing," say "One of Aunt Amy's favorite articles of clothing was her bright red polka-dotted dress that clung tightly to her figure and she often said made her look like a rock star! She loved to wear it with stiletto heels. And boy! Did she ever get the looks when she walked in a room!"
- End on a happy or upbeat note
- Thank people for coming

Don't be afraid to use humor. A funny story might be just what is needed to help people remember the character and life of your loved one. Make sure it puts her/him in a good light. Recently I attended a funeral in which the eulogist read two humorous poems that the deceased woman had written. Everyone laughed and thought that was exactly what she would have wanted to have read in her memory! For another example, read the eulogy written by John Cleese for his friend, Graham Chapman. Avoidance of humor would have been very inappropriate for an associate of John's and a fellow member of the Monty Python comedy troupe; this eulogy can be found online.

A eulogy gives a celebratory picture of the person who has died. There is a fine line between eulogizing and idealizing. Eulogies that are most moving recognize the foibles of the deceased and those things that they struggled with, but do so in a way that does not "tell tales out of school" and shares information in a tasteful manner.

Several people had spoken, eulogizing the matriarch of the community with kind words and acknowledging the achievements and contributions she had made to the community. When Reverend Davis stood up to talk about his old friend and foe, Hazel Huckvale, he did so by telling the true nature of their relationship. Hazel had been a feisty elder in the congregation. She always spoke her mind and she always had directions for the minister to follow. Reverend Davis told the stories with a smile on his face and he brought grins and nods from the full church because they knew he was also speaking of a real part of Hazel.

Often when struggles are talked about, it is in a way that shows how the person overcame or was working towards overcoming those issues. What not to say: "Mary struggled with mental illness all her life but in spite of it managed to be successful at hairdressing and even winning an award." In this example, Mary is seen through negative eyes instead of focusing on the positive and mentioning the mental illness in a subtle way. It would have been better to say: "Mary started her hairdressing salon in 1995 and worked through the challenges of running a business, raising a family on her own, and fighting mental illness. I still remember the excitement when she won the Hairdresser of the Year award."

DO

- Start with an attention getter
- Have a beginning, middle and end
- Tell stories to demonstrate the type of person s/he was
- Speak from the heart
- Speak positively about the deceased
- Use everyday language
- Use short sentences

DO NOT

- Bring up bad habits
- Give gory details
- Tell dirty stories
- Swear
- Ramble
- Forget your reading glasses
- Related facts and dates and events – tell stores about them
- Use formal written style
- Use jargon or acronyms that few people will understand
- Overuse cliches

Step 4: Practice Your Talk

Depending on your skill and comfort level, you will decide whether you will speak or read the eulogy. Some techniques that you can use to practice are:

- Read it aloud. Read it aloud to someone else. Listen for breaks, inaccuracies or repetitions. If your tongue trips over a phrase, reword it so that you can speak it easily.
- Read or say it into a digital recorder and play it back.
- Read or say it to yourself in front of a mirror.
- Go over your presentation several hours before you are to speak and then put it away and don't look at it again until it is time to stand up and speak. Give your mind a rest so that it can process the information.

Step 5: Have a Backup Plan

Enlist a support person.

Print out two copies of your speech. Give one to a trusted friend or family member who has agreed to read it if you are unable to do so. Rarely is this needed, but it will help you feel stronger knowing that you have a backup plan.

This would have alleviated the problem for the poor granddaughter who was to the last page of her eulogy and she realized she didn't have the final page!

She shuffled papers, looked around nervously and in the end, just said, "I don't have the rest" and sat down dejectedly.

If someone in the audience had a second copy, they could have gotten up and handed it to her and she could have carried on. She would not still be dismally remembering the day she lost the final page.

DO

- Put Kleenex in your pocket.
- Drink a glass of water before you start and have one close by while you are speaking. Drinking water helps you de-stress but do not drink so much that you have to take a bathroom break and find yourself out of the room when it is your turn to speak!
- Take a few deep breaths before standing up to have your say.
- Wear clothes and shoes that are comfortable and are not going to sidetrack you from what you are about to do. Your clothing should be neat and clean and convey your personality and your authoritativeness.
- Take a walk to calm yourself and to get in touch with those thoughts that are important to you. If you pray, this would be an opportunity to be alone and say your prayers. If you jog or run or workout regularly, make sure you don't forego this practice on the day of your presentation. It will help you stay calm.
- If you can comfortably do so, leave out points that have been spoken by the previous speaker.

    Recently I went to a funeral in which two speakers told the story of how the deceased had started a vital agency in the community. Both speakers had

84

plenty of other material. It would have been easy
for the second speaker to skip over that and just tell
his other stories.

DO NOT

- Take drugs (prescription or otherwise) to help you
  relax (at least not until after you have given your
  talk).
- Wear tight clothing that will restrict your ability to
  breathe or move freely.
- Worry if you cry. It is expected that you will be
  upset and emotional. Take time to recover and use
  your Kleenex, breathe deeply and take a drink of
  your water and then continue.

Remember, you are speaking to people that want to hear
the stories of this person you all loved. Whether you
speak, read, or cry, you will bring comfort to those
listening.

Perspectives from Two Ministers in the United Church of Canada

The Reverend Jenny Carter:

A eulogy needs to be about the person's life – not the details. A few good stories interspersed with why those particular stories are significant in the life of the person or their families are meaningful. The detail ones (born in such a year, died on this date, worked here...) are flippin' boring, and we're more than those details. A eulogy should tell the "story" of the person - what they loved, who they loved, what made them unique, what they valued. Also, making good use of metaphors can be powerful.

When planning the service of their loved one, people need to make the service reflective of the person. Don't choose hymns based on "Aunt Tilley's service 20 years ago" choose music that the person would have liked - or that the family likes. If listening to a song on a CD - just choose one. That's because the flow of the service, and people's attention span, can't handle more than that. Always, always, always, make the last song upbeat and hopeful. This is because people need to leave the service feeling better than when they came in (that's one of the reasons for having a service!).

When making use of PowerPoint (to view pictures etc.) it is wise to have this as part of the time of remembrance - that is where the eulogy and open mike time (if people choose to have that), go. I always put it at the end of those two things - it gives people a moment to pause and reflect on the person in light of what they heard shared in the eulogy. Plus, a good eulogy makes people chuckle and cry, and a good PowerPoint tends to make people just cry. It's wise to keep all of these grouped together. That is because the remainder of the service is meant to provide comfort and hope to the bereaved. It's very frustrating to get people comforted only to have them upset again because of a PowerPoint presentation at the end of the service.

Fill the worship space with things that are symbolic of the deceased person. Set up things that speak of their values, hobbies, activities, etc. Always have a picture of the person at the front (and it needs to be at least 8 1/2 x 11 inches). I always place a candle by the picture - a flame is alive and warm and reminiscent of the spirit - it helps bring the space to life.

I always encourage families to think of how they want to "memorialize" or "symbolically" say good bye during the service. This most often happens when they walk in. Many families choose to have each family member place a flower by the picture of their loved one. One family totally blew me away. The service was for the grandpa. He had been a house builder all of his life, and each family member had a piece of wood with their name on it. Two of the grandsons stood at the front, and as each family member came in, they handed these young men their piece of wood. The young men then set about placing the pieces together. When they stepped back, a little wooden house (made up of the individual pieces which represented everyone in the family) was revealed. At that very instant I changed my meditation - I had to. What I chose to speak about was how "love builds the house". That was powerful - and it came from the family.

Whoever is leading the service (and its best if ONE person has control over the flow of service and is responsible for leading most of it) needs to always have the last word. That means they speak last. This is because their only job is to offer comfort and hope - so they need to go after all of the things that tend to make people feel really sad. In addition, if somebody gets up and says something outrageous - which I have had happen - they need to be able to speak to it in some sensitive way. Otherwise the only thing people remember about the service is the offbeat, or strange, comment. That is why I tend to have all of the speeches and open mike stuff contained early on in the service during the "time of remembrance". That gives me the rest of the service to do what needs to be done in terms of comfort and hope. (Rev. Jenny Carter, personal communication, 11 May 2009)

The Reverend Karen Millard:

I agree with Jenny, I also would say I find that if I ask the family to tell me stories and memories they usually start out afraid, but I give them time to think and respond. I also try to ask kids as well so that they don't get excluded.

If no one is comfortable giving a reflection I always use stories that have been given me and make it all about that person. The family at the end needs to be able to say "Wow, it's like you knew him/her."

I also focus on the fact that the service is about those who are there grieving and ascertain what it is that they need. As Jenny said don't make it like Auntie Jane's funeral 25 years ago......

I always say to the family that has said "We don't want to do the eulogy" – "Let me know if you change your mind". I have a sample eulogy that I wrote for my grandmother that sometimes they like to read that helps people get started. I almost always have someone come to me at the end and say they would like to do the eulogy - in fact I think it has happened every time...when it comes to the day they are usually more ready to speak.

I also attempt to include names of closest family and friends in prayers...obviously including those who we have not named but people say it is very meaningful to be prayed for by name. (Rev. Karen Millard, personal communication, 11 May 2009)

The Reverend Jenny Carter:

Thanks for the reminder Karen. I too always start my time with the family by getting them to share stories of the person. This not only helps me get a handle on who that person was, it gives me insight into the family dynamics and how they are experiencing their grief. This leads to a better service and a reflection/meditation that people will find helpful and comforting. Before writing my reflection I always ask the deceased person "what do your loved ones need to hear" - and then I always make sure I go to the hard stuff in a soft way. (Rev. Jenny Carter, personal communication, 11 May 2009)

The Reverend Ted Bristow

A good rule to remember if you want a simple short eulogy is to pick and elaborate on one feature of the person everyone would recognize as a memory to keep and an example to follow. (Rev. Ted Bristow, personal communication, 17 April 2009)

Writing a Difficult Eulogy

There will be times when a person with whom you had great difficulties dies and yet the eulogy still falls upon your shoulders. Think carefully about what you say and how you say it. What were the challenges as opposed to the problems? What did people learn from the experience? How can you celebrate the life without allowing the behavior to mar the picture?

Sample Eulogies

A Son to His Father

I have included as an example a eulogy that was said by a son about his father. This was never a good relationship and most of the family had difficulties. After this talk was made, the sisters rushed up to their brother and said, "You said what we couldn't say. Thank you. We feel better."

In my reality I saw my father as a stern and honest man. He tried to do his best and sometimes he was successful. Just like all of us. What did I learn from him? To try and be more patient, to consider the answers on more than one level, to keep an open mind and, above all, a love of travel and new places.

Did I always understand and agree with what he did? No, I did not. When I was in grade one he forced me to learn the multiplication table. I was in tears but he was unrelenting. Not until much later did I appreciate the gift

91

*he had given me. I have the multiplication table ingrained
in me to use and call upon instantaneously. This may seem
a small and irrelevant thing but it illustrates my father's
attention to detail, and his tenacity to stick with the job
until it was done. I believe that Dick and Rhonda knew
about that when he came to visit them in Liverpool to help
them renovate their house.*

How do I phrase what I will say next?

*Toward his later years he became more withdrawn, less
tolerant of company and more confused in his thinking. It
was sad to see him deteriorate. The last time I saw him I
took his hand. The warmth flowed through his body; three
times I made to withdraw yet he held on to my hand. I
could not refuse.*

*It was not for me to question his journey. He had his
program. And as we all struggle through our own program,
wondering if we are on the right way, remember that Jesus
talks a lot about forgiveness. And so I will leave you with a
quote from the illustrious Koran: "Allah is merciful and
most forgiving."*

Thank you for coming.

When a Child Has Died

Losing a child is one of the most painful experiences that a
family can experience. If you have agreed to give the
eulogy for a child, you have taken on a very honorable and

difficult task. Attending the funeral or memorial service will be difficult for people to bear. Your words will be painful and at the same time comforting. Prepare yourself well, have your own support system to help you through this.

When you have been asked to speak at the service of a little one, begin your eulogy with your condolences to the family. Address the pain of the situation at the beginning of the eulogy and then focus on the love and happiness that was in this child's life – or for a very young one – for the love and happiness and hope that this child brought to the parents and grandparents. Talk about the relationships between parents and child and siblings and child so that the loved ones hear their names.

Thank you for coming and sharing this very difficult time with us. It is with very heavy heart that I stand before you to honor the memory of our child, Pippi Longstocking. She was only 12 years old when the tragic accident took the life of our wonderful friend, daughter, sister and cousin from us. We cannot even attempt to understand the why. My name is Melvin Thorpe and I am Pippi's favorite uncle. I am here today to share a few wonderful memories with you and to sadly say goodbye.

Pippi loved to do things differently. She thought it was great fun to have dessert first and was always egging her brother and sisters on to get mom to feed them ice cream first. "Then," she would say "if we are very good and eat all our ice cream up, we'll be rewarded with broccoli and chicken." She loved school and had lots of friends. They were always coming and going through the house. She liked to read stories aloud to her little friends and she was quite a story teller even without a book in front of her. Just this September Pippi received a puppy for a birthday present. Everyone knew how much she wanted a pet. She would feed and walk the neighbor's dog and when she received the present she was overjoyed. She taught Dudley to sit and to speak and she was still working on 'stay'. It will be up to Janie and Ian to finish that job now. We'll always remember Pippi in her pigtails and big grin.

To Mommy in Heaven – Words of Sympathy

Mommy, don't cry, 'cause God is holding my hand
and telling me everything is OK.

Mommy, God said that I will never want for anything
and I will still feel your love all the way up here.

Mommy, you should see me,
I am running and playing with God's other children.

Mommy, guess who helps watch over us while we play?
They are God's Helping Angels!

Mommy, I'm not afraid, my grandpa and grandma are here.
They came to me when it was dark and held my hands;
then we went to God's bright light,
where Angels were singing.

Mommy, God said, If you feel sad, to remember this;
I'll be the gentle breeze that brushes your face,
the sun is my smile and the rain is me washing
away your pain.

Mommy, I have to go now.
I send you all my love on the wings of an Angel.

Love from your son/daughter, to you Mommy.
(by Sandra L. Garman)

Sample Eulogies

Roberta Alexis (Taylor) Farmer was born in Maple Bay on January 23, 1950 and died one week ago on July 12th. She was my best friend and my sister. With heavy heart I am here today to honor her memory and give her a good send off. I want you to know the kind of person my sister was.

When we were growing up, we always shared a bedroom. Her bed was on one side of the room and mine was on the other. My side was usually messy and the bed strewn with books and clothes. Bobbi's side of the room was neat as a pin. She had 17 dolls that lived on her bed and slept with her every night when we were little. She would make sure that every one of them was comfortable before settling in herself. While I was busy reading under the covers with my flashlight, Bobbi was crooning to her babies!

She loved cooking and often had tea parties for family and friends. Her dolls were always present as well. Her favorite menu was tea with Lemon Cake that she learned how to make when she was quite young with the help of Grandma Virginia. I thought it was great fun to attend her tea parties and I think that she put up with me but I really was an irritating little sister back then.

As teenagers, we both became interested in boys and used to fight over which movie star we would marry when we got older. Bobbi liked to wear short skirts and makeup but our mother wasn't having any of that. Bobbi would leave the house dressed in the manner that mom approved, but by the time we got to the end of the street, she would have hiked up her skirt and the eye makeup came out of her bag and she would walk and make up her face. As I was a year and a half younger, I took all this in and learned some valuable lessons! Pretty soon, we were holding the mirror for each other.

Bobbi graduated from high school and thought that perhaps she would take a year off to travel the world on our parents' expense account, but Dad was having none of that. He promised Bobbi instead that once she had received a bachelor's degree he would pay for a summer in Europe. She took him up on that and finished her BSc in 1972 without too many incidents and enjoyed trekking around Europe for 3 months. It was a time when she made some good friends and came back with ideas for her future. She also came back with an engagement ring on her finger!

Bobbi got a job teaching home economics at the local high school and the first summer after coming back from Europe there was a wedding. It was a beautiful wedding at the Community Hall in our community. I was so proud of my sister and how beautiful she looked in her homemade gown with the hand-beaded top that she had designed and sewn herself! I had also made my bridesmaid gown but I didn't have the skills or the patience that Bobbi had.

Bobbi didn't give up teaching right away. She taught for another 3 years before she and Rod decided to start their own family. They had purchased a house on the Ridge – not too far from Mom and Dad – and their future looked rosy. And it was! In the next few years, three wonderful gifts of God arrived: Teddy, Celia and Katie. Now she could put all the skills that she had been practicing as a child on those 17 dolls to work. I think she did a great job! Now those three are wonderful young adults with families and careers of their own.

She was a great mom as I know Teddy, Celia and Katie will tell you. And she's even a greater grandma! As a mom, she was sewing dance costumes, volunteering at the skating rink and cheering on Teddy on the soccer field. She helped out with the homework – never doing it for her children but asking questions, supplying study materials and being a cheer leader. And for the last few years she has been using those same skills to bring joy to her grandchildren, Tyler, Roni, Brittany and Ben. Have you seen the baby quilts she has made? Phenomenal!

When Katie graduated, Bobbi decided it was time to go back to her teaching degree. She had been substituting for home economics teachers for the past five years but now was her chance to take on the head of the department and really get into her career. In 1999 she won the School District Award for Most Innovating Teaching. After six years, Bobbi discovered that she had cancer. She finished out the school year and gave her resignation.

Over the past 5 years that Bobbi has lived with cancer, she and Rod have travelled to Australia, Fuji, Japan, Thailand, and she revisited parts of her European trip in the 70's. Bobbi's favorite spot was Costa Rica and she often talked about what it would be like to spend the rest of her life on a private little beach in that country. I'm glad she didn't – I would have been robbed of these past few years when our relationship flourished even more than in the past. My husband, Don and I took several trips with Rod and Bobbi. We got together often for BBQs and other family events. What would Christmas, Thanksgiving and other holidays be like without Bobbi's signature turkey dressing? I will miss her so much!

Even though Bobbi knew that the cancer was going to kill her, she did not let that stop her from living. Travelling, spending time with her family, and generally enjoying life became her priority. She is a true role model to all who knew her.

If I could use three words to sum up my sister's life they would be Caring, Fun and Efficient! *Having a sister is like having a best friend you can't get rid of. You know whatever you do, they'll still be there* (Amy Li). Well you have gone in body, but I know you will never leave me spiritually. Bobbi, I will miss you here to play with – but I know that your spirit lives on within our family and especially in the lives of your 4 grandchildren.

Hello, my name is Ted – even though Aunt Sharon calls me Teddy. I wanted to share with you some of the stories of my childhood which will tell you what a wonderful mother I had.

I was the only boy on the soccer field who came to practice with homemade cupcakes for the team. My mother would "whip" up something for the team to celebrate a win, a loss, a tie and even a practice. I was known for having the neatest mom! Both my parents were always at my practices and my games.

One time when I was in my teens I got really sick. I was home for ages. I didn't go to the hospital but I know that people were concerned about me. I remember my mother sleeping beside my bed on the cot she had my dad haul into my room. She said she just wanted to be near me in case I needed her in the night.

But she wasn't controlling, and she didn't try to know everything about my life. She gave me freedom along with cupcakes! I remember my sisters and I deciding when we were little that we were going to go into the lemonade stand business. We reassured our mom that we were big enough to know what we were doing. We built the stand with leftover boards and made a paper sign. Then we made the lemonade – I think it was lemon Kool-aid – and we set out to sell it. We were very proud of ourselves and we were proud of the fact that we had done it all by ourselves without the help of our mom. I'm not sure how many customers we had – a few from up and down the road. We took our profits to the corner store and bought penny candy with it. I remember we went to bed with tummy aches that night!

When I was a teenager, I got into a bit of trouble. My mom was there to help me straighten it out. Instead of being mad and yelling at me like I was worried about, she quietly sat on the edge of my bed – in my room – and had a private little chat with me about the consequences of my actions. The way she talked it made so much sense to me, I only tried my wild ways a few more times before I accepted her wisdom. I wasn't an angel; I had to try some stuff on my own. Her wisdom and guidance, I think, were what kept me from getting myself into a lot of trouble.

When I met Elaine I brought her home to meet "Mom" and the two of them liked each other immediately. Instead of awkward silences between my parents and my girlfriend, Mom took Elaine and gave her a tour of the house – showed Elaine her quilting and sewing projects and then out to the garden for a glass of ice tea – just the women! Thank goodness! Elaine and I are married now and have two children and wonderful memories of my mother.

My mother will be missed.

Eulogy for an Aunt. (This 9-minute eulogy was a part of several eulogies given that day. It has been translated from Dutch into English.)

Dearest Win and all other family and friends of Margot. First of all from this place I would like to offer my sincere sympathy in your loss, to let you know that I am really sad with the loss that you have suffered.

Win, when you called me with the question, "Would you like to say something?" I wondered if I could or would want to do that. I wondered, were my contacts with Margot something I could tell others about? But then you said that you would really appreciate it if I would speak, and that under no circumstances should it be a sad or sober speech. In that I recognized my feelings towards the loss of your mother and knew that I wanted to say something. Everybody knew Margot through their own eyes and their own experience and I am simply a modest part in her life. Actually she has always been my Auntie Margot - the wife of Uncle Theo who is the blood brother of my father.

Our families didn't see each other that often but as a child I often found it exciting to visit your family in Scheveningen. There you had fun! It was laissez-faire and cozy. And Win, you don't know how much I appreciated it when you recently told me how much you enjoyed it as well. It was comforting to know that our feelings were mutual.

Afterwards many things changed in our circumstances. We were too busy, so to speak, to get together and this resulted in our having too little contact with each other. Our only contact most of the time was that which was kept alive by our mothers writing letters to each other.

A few years ago I picked up the phone and called Margot. We had so much to talk about and everyone who knew Margot can imagine that we had an hour-long conversation without even trying to think about what we might talk about. It was an award winning conversation!

Out of that we concluded that we both shared a passion for computers. We immediately made an appointment for a marathon session. We had fun discussing in detail the excitement of our hobby. In the meantime we exchanged ideas and shared programs. From that moment on, Margot was not only my Aunt but my computer mate.

She was youthful and dynamic. It was in the 1980's. She kept wanting to improve and learn more and come hell or high water she wanted to get that computer under control.

I don't think that anyone would be surprised to hear that Margot has taught me in a short time more about how to word process than I would have been able to learn from books. It would have taken me weeks to get the same information out of books. She really encouraged me.

There was no feeling of age difference between us and on the basis of equal mates we spent a lot of hours on the computer. Every now and again we would have a break and have a nice meal at a cozy restaurant. When I showed her a computer program for genealogy, this really spoke to her and from that moment on our contact became even more frequent.

Because of her ability to really delve into something – in any subject, in this case genealogy, with the help of family and friends –she managed to collect a fortune of information specifically about my side of the family. This is something I am very grateful for.

Of course this program was, in her eyes, incomplete. And so she designed her own program to do what she wanted it to do.

A short while ago when she already knew that her illness was terminal, she called me up. About her situation, she would only make brief comments; that wasn't why she would call. She was very irritated about her printer and she had absolutely for the rest of her life to 'be annoyed to no end with such a stupid piece of mechanics' and would I please get her another printer. And "oh yes, my hard drive is too small – could you do something about that too?"

She remarked about the time crisis in which she found herself. She wanted to complete all these tasks before she died.

In this that was her trademark "the little giant", Margot advised to never give up, as much as possible decide your own destiny, and never, never, never, never, have self pity.

Margot stays in my memory as immovable, indestructible, determined with vision and with an innate ability to put words on paper. I'm very thankful for having known Margot and wish strength to all that loved this little big woman.

When I wrote the eulogy for my mother's funeral I had a rich store of tales to tell. My mother was a natural storyteller and I had heard the stories of her youth all my life. My mother had a great number of experiences before I was born to her when she was 38 years old. She had been in World War II, she had been a Customs Officer, she had lived in a Roman Catholic convent, she had gone to Art School, and she had had a number of men friends throughout those years before finally finding the right man a year before I was born!

I sat down and thought "What are the important parts of her life that she would want me to remind people of?" and "What are those parts of her that I think it is important for people to hear about from my perspective?" What parts of her life am I proud of?

And then I put her stories together with my remembrances and had a historical and loving tribute to the 83 years that my mother lived on this earth. Some of the stories were sad (the man who was the love of her life and had taken her 38 years to find died after only 9 short years of marriage), some heartwarming (the day the Newfoundland dock was filled with relatives greeting her as she came in by boat to visit) and several humorous (the time she picked blackberries and then mailed them to her father; they dripped juice all the way from her house to his.)

I didn't write the eulogy out. I just jotted down points to direct me on a recipe card, which I ended up not even referring to when I stood up to speak (but I could have). It was a topic I knew so well and had been a student of every day of my life.

Don't worry about details that don't add to the story.

Her father was in a sanatorium for tuberculosis in a city 300 miles from the family home. My mother stayed with Aunt Janie in a rural area several miles from the family home during the summer. All that really needs to be said is "Mom stayed with her Aunt Janie on the farm during this time." Too many details and worrying about exact facts only drag down the story.

"Whenever I visited my mother I could not go empty handed. To arrive without her favorite box of chocolates only meant that I was thoughtless and that we would have to put on our coats and go to the Chocolate shop as the first thing we did." Even though I am speaking about my own experience, the central character in this anecdote is

my mother. I am giving the listeners a picture of my mother and her love of sweets and expectations of her daughter's visit.

Eulogy Template

Use this as a guide in case of emergency.

(*Name*); (*date of birth*) at (*place of birth*) to (*date of death*) of (*cause of death*) at (*place of death*).

We are gathered here today because we knew and loved (*common name used*) and we want to celebrate his/her life. My name is (*name*) and I was (*name of deceased*)'s (*relationship to the deceased*). Each person here today has their own memories of (*name of deceased*). It is with honor and great sorrow that I stand here to share with you my memories. It means a great deal to the whole family that you have been able to be with us today.

(*Name*) grew up in (*name of place or places, i.e. third son*) in a family of (*number of siblings*). His/her parents were (*names of parents*) (*profession/occupation of parents*), and his/her brothers and sisters (*names of the family members*) are here with us today. (*Deceased's name*) had a great love of (*music, hockey, doing good for others, making the world a better place, etc.*) throughout his/her life. We will all remember her/him for her/his (*accomplishments/adventures/time spent*) in this area. (*Add a sentence or story here about this.*)

During his/her growing up years (*name*) (*was happy,
endured many challenges, enjoyed life to the fullest, was
studious, enjoyed family activities*). As a child (*name*)
loved to (*activity*). At school (*name*) (*excelled/was
dedicated, was bored/did well without trying*) because
she/he (*loved to learn/valued education and was looking
ahead to a strong career based on his/her
education/preferred to do practical things/wanted to be
outside playing and having adventures*). The things that
he/she loved to do the best were
(*art/mathematics/drama/sports/annoying his/her
teachers/hanging out with his/her friends
(names)/daydreaming about the future/writing love
letters/romantic poetry*). His/her motto for that time in
his/her life might have been (*s/he who works hard gets
ahead/life is too short not to party/daydreaming is the
source of the future*).

One story about (*name of deceased*) goes this way: (*story
from their growing up years. You could add one or two
more here if you have them. They could include stories of
school, sports, extracurricular activities or home.*)

(*Name of deceased*) (*graduated/left school*) and as a young
adult and went on to (*college, university, the military, first
job, to get married*). A highlight of that time of his/her life
was (*story you have/getting a degree/making
money/achieving fame/getting a medal/fighting on the front
lines/meeting future spouse/other*).

(*Name*)'s career throughout his/her life was (*engineering/fishing/being a homemaker, wife and mother/teaching*) and that brought him/her (*great joy/frustrated him/her/was a job that he/she did until he/she found his/her passion in later life/received great acclaim in/made a difference to the world because of*) (*Here is where you could insert a story or two about this person and their career.*)

(*Name*) had (*many/several/one*) close friends over the years and (*someone/some people*) who were particularly significant in (*name*)'s life (*was/were*) (*names*). (*Name*) from (*school, work, other*) meant a great deal to (*name*) and they spent many hours together (*playing Scrabble/traveling the world/studying together at university/helping the poor in India*). (*Add a story here if you have one*).

If the person was married:

(*Name*) met (*his/her*) (*first*) husband/wife during (*school/university/other*) in (*year*) and it was (*love at first sight/a long courtship/sparks flying from the first*). (*Story of how they met in 2 sentences*). They (*have been/were*) married for (*number*) years. They had (*number*) children: (*names in order of birth*) and (*name*) was so proud of them and loved them so deeply. (*Story here about the children*).

In later years, (*name*) became a grand (*father/mother*) of (*names in order of birth*) and was even prouder of this accomplishment. The grandchildren were a source of continuous joy and pride! (*Story here if you have one about the children*).

As many people have reminded me over the past few days, (*name*) was a (*list his/her character traits*). One of my fondest memories of (*name*) is the time that (*story to emphasize the character trait*).

(*Name*) was a good (*husband/wife, great father/mother*), beloved grandparent and the best friend a person could have, and he/she will be greatly missed by all of us.

(*Name*)'s death was (*sudden/not sudden*) and even though we were (*prepared/unprepared*) we are here together today to mourn the loss of our friend and loved one here on earth. Coming together to celebrate her/his life will also be a way that will begin the healing process for all of us. As Terrence Rattigan, one of England's most popular 20th century dramatists stated: "I will not insult you by trying to tell you that one day you will forget. I know as well as you that you will not. But, at least, in time you will not remember as fiercely as you do now – and I pray that that time may be soon." Jack Lemmon said "Death ends a life, not a relationship." I wish us all wonderful memories and continued relationship with (*name*).

Chapter 5: Understanding Feelings of Grief and Loss

My poor sad face and garb must tell its tale.
Queen Victoria

Definitions from the Merriam-Webster Dictionary

Grief: a deep and poignant distress.

Sorrow: deep distress, sadness, or regret especially for the loss of someone or something loved.

Mourning: an outward sign (as black clothes or an armband) of grief for a person's death; a period of time during which signs of grief are shown.

Bereaved: suffering the loss of a loved one.

Tears: an act of weeping of grieving.

Understanding and Managing Your Grief

You cannot describe grief in a checklist or a bulleted itemized statement. This feeling that takes over your life when a significant loss occurs is more than just a list of symptoms and remedies. It is an experience that fills up your whole being. It stops you, overwhelms you, confuses you, and drives your actions or inactions.

There is no trite description that fits for everyone or that will tell you how you will feel, how long you will feel it, or even when you will start to feel your life returning to normal. Grieving takes place when we have a loss; it could be for a job, a way of life, the death of a pet, a move, the end of a marriage or other relationship, or the death of a dear friend or relative.

The thought of living on this earth without your loved one can be horrifying. Our physical, mental and emotional systems react to the loss. Professionals who have worked with the bereaved have observed the stages that people go through after a loss and have identified stages that will help you to realize that you are not alone – you are going through natural processes. And yet, even with these natural stages, we will react depending on our own personal makeup. How we react depends on many factors: our ability to deal with stress and our coping style, our personality type, our culture, our upbringing, our physical and mental health.

The first few days after receiving the news of your loss of a loved one can be very draining and debilitating. A woman whose husband was killed in a crash said to me "I'm dazed and stunned. I don't believe it and yet how can I think that the police are lying to me." And this was after she and her brother-in-law had identified the body of her husband. When a death is sudden, your bereavement may be more complicated. Your feelings of disbelief and unbelief may grow stronger. However, even if you are like Kirk, you may feel surprised and overwhelmed. Kirk knew his father was dying and he thought that he was prepared for death, and when his father died he told me "I thought it would be easier for me because I have sat by his bed and watched him fade away. But when he died, I was still shocked, I was still upset, I was still angry that he had left me!"

Janice and Stu had been married for 35 years. Stu had just arrived home as the phone was ringing. It took a minute or two for him to realize that Janice was not answering the phone so he reached for the one in the hallway near the door. It was his sister, Marg. She said "Stu, there has been an accident." And in that moment, Stu's life changed forever. He wondered if she could be joking. He wondered if Janice would walk through the door and say "Ha! Got ya'!" He was irritated. "Stop goofing around, sis!" But Marg was not joking. Janice had been run over as she crossed a busy downtown street. She died before she got to the hospital. "It just can't be" thought Stu and he slumped to the floor, the first waves of grief washing over him.

Three months later, Stu is still waking up and expecting Janice to be sleeping next to him. His first thoughts are of her until he rolls over and finds her missing. He is still startled and then sad when he realizes that Janice is gone.

Because grief can be so painful, so overwhelming at times, people can become frightened and concerned if they are grieving in the "right" way. People wonder if the feelings they have are normal. Whether a person has lost a job, a way of life, a partner, a loved one or even a pet, grief is a normal process which will happen no matter how hard one may try to ignore it.

There are healthy ways to deal with grief and to help the process. It is important to know what can happen.

Most grieving people may have one or more of the following physical sensations:

- Tightness in the throat
- Heaviness in the chest
- Appetite loss
- Empty feeling in the stomach
- Sensations of being in the old situation
- Difficulty sleeping
- Loss of energy
- Over-abundance of energy
- The need to sigh
- Choking
- Shortness of breath
- Uncontrollable crying

Feelings and emotions can be intense and can include any of these experiences:

- Sense of unreality
- Guilt
- Anger
- Regret for what did or didn't happen

- Unpredictable mood swings
- Anguish
- Sadness
- Depression
- Loneliness
- Shock
- Numbness
- Relief
- Confusion
- Irritability

Behavior changes can be confusing. At times a person can feel like they are going crazy from the mood swings and the different way of acting now in grief, such as:

- Feeling restless
- Looking for an activity but finding it difficult to concentrate
- Wandering aimlessly
- Forgetting or not finishing projects
- Dreaming frequently of the old ways
- Becoming intensely preoccupied with life the way it used to be
- Having a need to protect others from being uncomfortable by not talking about one's grief
- Feeling a diminished sense of self-worth with the loss of the familiar role (husband, wife, parent, child, friend)

Spiritual and philosophical issues may trouble a grieving person. You might be:

- Questioning your understanding of God, the system, the world or life
- Asking "Why me?"
- Feeling angry with God, the system, the world or life
- Thinking life is unfair

These responses are normal and natural.

It helps to cry and to talk with non-judgmental friends when you need to. Here are some other things that you can do when you are grieving:

- Keep yourself around people who care about you. Do not shut yourself off from your support group. If you do not have a support group, reach out to people who care and invite them to spend time with you.

- Talk to them. Tell them how you feel.

- Ask for help when you need it.

- Accept help from others.

- Journal, create, play the piano, or find another outlet that helps you expend your creative energy through this process. (For example, one person I know becomes a poet anytime they are feeling upset or are grieving.) Note: You don't need to save what you write or draw or create. The purpose is to use your emotions and let them out. Sometimes it helps to wad up the paper filled with words or images and toss it vigorously into the trash, a symbol of throwing away the anger.

- Take time for yourself. Sometimes getting out by yourself and looking at peaceful scenes such as a flower garden, walking on the beach, going to a museum to view rich colors or having a quiet time at a local church, chapel or synagogue can bring relief.

- Don't be afraid to cry

- Take the time you need to mourn or grieve. No one can tell you a "normal" period of time for this process.

- Look after your physical health and eat properly and exercise regularly. Swimming laps, golfing, walking, scrubbing the floor, waxing the car or furniture, trimming bushes or making bread help vent intense feelings.

- Avoid drugs and alcohol. They only dull the pain you must feel to do your grief work.

- Join a grief support group if it's right for you.

- Don't let people tell you it's time to stop grieving or get on with your life before you are ready.

- You may find yourself forgetful or absent minded. This is normal. Keep a list of things that you need to do at this time to make sure the important things in your life get done. This is especially true around the time of the funeral. Carry the list around with you. Jot down things as you think of them. This also can include keeping lists of schedules, callers and appointments marked on calendars.

- Look after others in their grief.

- If you are having trouble working through this on your own, enlist the help of a grief counselor. For example: When Sarah's ex-husband died she felt it was wrong to grieve for a man she had been divorced from for 10 years. She went to see a grief counselor who gave her permission to mourn. Instead of feeling guilty, she could then focus on the sense of loss that she felt for the father of her children and the man who had played a large role in her life for 35 years.

- Postpone any major decisions for a year. For instance, if your spouse has died, don't sell your house, jump into a new relationship or move across the country until you have had time to grieve. Making a major decision at this time can cause you more stress. It can also create a bigger margin for error as your focus is on the loss and does not allow you to use the same judgment that you would if you were not in the grieving process.

- Work towards acceptance. Work toward starting a new life with new relationships and new plans.

Working through grief takes a long time. Be patient with yourself.

When Addison's husband died, she withdrew from the people that she normally socialized with and stayed home in her garden and did an inordinate amount of crosswords and weeding. When Jamie's husband died she played solitaire on the computer and thought of nothing. When Al's wife died he joined a walking group and spent as much time as he could walking in nature. When Charlie's wife died he travelled the globe for the first year, visiting places he had always meant to see and meeting a lot of new people.

Donald lost his wife and Marti started bringing over suppers; they spent long evenings talking about the meaning of life. Wendy's mother died and she said "I walked around in a daze" for months, I felt numb for a long time.

Linda and Grace were good friends and talked on the phone daily. Linda died suddenly. For months after Linda's death, Grace found herself picking up the phone to call Linda to tell her the latest news and then she would look at the phone and a strong sense of loss would engulf her as she realized Linda was no longer there to answer her call.

When Cyndi's sister died, she refused to stop doing all that she was doing; she said she loved her sister but didn't have time to mourn. When I spoke to Cyndi she told me this: *Three years later, I sat down one day with a plunk! And that is when I stopped doing and started grieving. I took a year off from everything: work, church, helping out with the neighborhood watch program. Even my family was told to do Christmas on their own that year. I spent a lot of time on my own remembering my sister, talking out loud to her in case she could hear. I yelled at her for a while too. I read, I crocheted, I cleaned my house from attic to basement and then I painted everything I'd cleaned. I felt like I went into this dark hole and then as I re-emerged I cleaned and painted my way out! My husband put up with me through this whole time. What a love! I'm ok now, but it was a really tough year ... and the three years before that? Well, I just ignored the pain. I thought I was invincible and that I could just "get over it". Boy was I wrong!*

Helping Children with their Grief

When my father died, I was seven years old, I grieved and all around me people were saying how strong I was and how resilient children were. I grieved and thought my life would never be the same again. I was missing something vital to my world. My mother went for coffee with a male friend and I panicked. I threw a tantrum! It was only ten months after my father's death and I immediately jumped to the conclusion that this man was going to be brought in to replace my father. I was wrong, but I was panic stricken! And my poor mother didn't understand – she thought I was just being a spoiled child!

A program called Rainbows helps children identify their feelings and discuss their grief with a trained leader and others of their age group. There are Rainbow non-profit groups in Australia, Canada, UK, Ireland, and the United States and, as their brochure states, they have "a history of successfully restoring hope to those who have suffered the pain of loss." Children need someone they can trust to offer guidance as they encounter the stages of grief and belonging to a weekly group in which they can speak and listen and understand that they are not alone or abnormal is very important. The sessions are designed for specific age groups from age three through to high school. If you do not find them through your funeral home or church, you can contact them at their website http://www.rainbows.org.

Stages of Grief and Loss

From "On Death and Dying"   by Elizabeth Kubler-Ross

These are the stages of grief you may experience.

Denial

"I feel fine."; "This can't be happening, not to me!"

Anger

"Why me? It's not fair!"; "How can this happen to me!" "Who is to blame?"

Bargaining

"Just let me live to see my children graduate."; "I'll do anything for a few more years."; "I will give my life savings if..."

Depression

"I'm so sad, why bother with anything?"; "I'm going to die . What's the point?"; "I miss my loved one, why go on?"

Acceptance

"It's going to be okay."; "I can handle it with change"; "I can't fight it, I may as well prepare for it."

There is no set pattern for when each stage happens or how long it will last. Some may be repeated.

Chapter 6: Public Speaking Tips for the Eulogist

"Be sincere; be brief; be seated." -
Franklin D. Roosevelt

Your loved one or close friend has just died, and you are going to give a speech. If you are afraid, you are not alone. It is a well-known fact that people fear public speaking more than they fear flying. Depending on the study between 40% − 70% of people claim that public speaking is their fear. Right now you have a job to do for someone you have loved very much. It is important to deal with your fear and use this guide to help you give proper tribute to the one you love.

One of the basics of public speaking is having a well-written speech.

Have your speech prepared at least a few days prior to presenting it. Listen to your speech a couple of times a day leading up to delivering the speech.

You can also practice in these places:

- in front of a mirror
- to a friend
- in front of a video camera
- at the place the speech will be given

Benjamin Franklin (1706-1790) said it well: *By failing to prepare you are preparing to fail.*

Pat Nichol, public speaking guru, says: *If you are a new public speaker, write everything that you have to say in 18 – 20 point font. Print it out and take your papers with you. Put them on the podium and take the podium in both hands and read.*

1. Number the pages.

2. Make two copies and give one of the copies to a close friend who can take over if you are unable to continue. Attach your copies together so that you don't lose a page. You can staple them or put a hole through the top corner and tie with a string.

3. Read this through several times aloud to yourself, in front of a mirror and to someone who loves you.

4. Don't worry about being perfect or having all the details.

5. Don't memorize your whole eulogy, but it is a good idea to memorize your opening 2 or 3 sentences. Without a doubt, the opening for any speech or presentation is the most difficult aspect of presenting. Getting through your opening smoothly, flawlessly, and without hesitation will increase your confidence and make the rest of your delivery easier.

6.   Relax and visualize your success. If you close your eyes and visualize yourself successfully delivering the speech, you will literally trick your brain into believing you've done it before and you won't feel as nervous. Use positive affirmations to tell yourself you will honor your loved one in a good way.

7.   Don't wear heavy or tight-fitting garments. Make sure you wear clothing that breathes. Polyesters and other man-made fabrics don't breathe and will make you sweat all the more. Choose natural fabrics such as cotton, wool, silk, and linen for optimum breathing ability. Make sure you have washed and pressed your outfit and there are no coffee or soup stains.

8.   Arrive early. Make sure you know the set-up of the room. Make any adjustments that you need to make in order to be prepared. Greet people as they arrive; even though that is not your job it will help you to have already engaged with your audience.

9.   Don't drink alcohol before speaking.

10.   Take a glass of water to the podium with you. (If you are talking on Zoom, be sure your glass of water is well away from the computer keyboard!)

11.   Be sure to introduce yourself. Once people understand who you are and how you fit in, they can then concentrate on your words. I have missed the meaning

of some of the references in a eulogy when I haven't known who was giving them.

12. Have several tissues with you.

13. Use variety in your voice when you speak and allow your facial expression and body language to further enhance your delivery.

14. Hand gestures should match the spoken words. Never put them in your pockets because you can't use them. Rest your hands lightly on the lectern; they are then ready to be used to enhance the speech.

15. Even if you are reading the eulogy, be sure to make eye contact with your audience. Stop and look around at crucial moments. You can even write the instructions into your speech – just make sure you put it in brackets or highlight it so that you remember not to read "make eye contact" to the audience. When you make eye contact you engage with your audience, you make them feel welcome, you let those listening know that you are confident and that you know your material, and it shows that you are sincere, friendly, credible and honest. It will help in the healing process of those present because the listeners hear that they are not alone in their grief and in their love of the deceased.

16. When you are telling stories about the deceased, tell the story rather than read it even if you have it written

down. The listeners will appreciate you deviating from the written script to look up at them and tell a story that sounds off the cuff and an easy memory.

17. Use appropriate props to help focus you and your audience. For example: You might want to talk about the fact that your Uncle spent a lot of time chairing meetings and at one point in his career was awarded a golden gavel. You could pick this gavel up when you begin to tell this story. At my mother's memorial service, I used a box of chocolates as a prop to make a point about our relationship and then at the conclusion of the eulogy I circulated through the chapel and passed out chocolates to everyone.

18. Don't talk too fast. Less is more here too. Pauses are effective.

19. Don't apologize for your speech or for your nerves. The audience will be hoping you succeed. Just have the intention of doing your best.

20. Your nervousness is normal, and others may not even know you are nervous if you don't tell them.

21. Take yourself seriously if you want your audience to. Speak with conviction, enthusiasm and sincerity. If you feel that you are going to cry – or that your voice is breaking, don't worry – people will expect that. Stop, take a breath, take a drink of water and carry on when you are ready.

22.   More and more people are using PowerPoint these days. If you use a PowerPoint presentation, do not write out what you are going to say on the slides. Use the slides to show pictures that illustrate your words.

23.   Use the area in which you are standing to your advantage. If it helps to move, walk back and forth as you speak. If you choose to stay behind the podium to read your speech, think of it as a protective shield.

Chapter 7: Quotes and Readings

*Many cultures identify mourning as the
very source of poetry and music, what
Elizabeth Bishop calls the art of losing.*
                              Peter Washington

Resources for the Eulogy: Quotes and Poetry

In this section I have included some poetry and quotes that
you can use in your eulogy, on the cover of your order of
service or wherever else it might fit.

When we lose a friend we die a little. Robert Herrick
(1591-1674)

What the heart has known, it shall never forget. (Anon)

She is Gone   David Harkins, Silloth, Cumbria

*Words from the poem on the Order of Service for the
Queen Mother's funeral*

You can shed tears that she is gone
Or you can smile because she has lived

You can close your eyes and pray that she will come back
Or you can open your eyes and see all that she has left

Your heart can be empty because you can't see her
Or you can be full of the love that you shared

You can turn your back on tomorrow and live yesterday
Or you can be happy for tomorrow because of yesterday

You can remember her and only that she is gone
Or you can cherish her memory and let it live on

 You can cry and close your mind, be empty and turn your
back

Or you can do what she would want: smile, open your eyes,
love and go on.

*The essence of every faith consists of its giving life a
meaning which death cannot destroy.* Leo Tolstoy (1828-
1910)

On Death Kahlil Gibran

You would know the secret of death.
But how shall you find it unless you seek it in the heart of
life?

The owl whose night-bound eyes are blind unto the day
cannot unveil the mystery of light.

If you would indeed behold the spirit of death, open your
heart wide unto the body of life.

For life and death are one, even as the river and the sea are
one.

In the depth of your hopes and desires lies your silent
knowledge of the beyond;

And like seeds dreaming beneath the snow your heart dreams of spring.

Trust the dreams, for in them is hidden the gate to eternity. Your fear of death is but the trembling of the shepherd when he stands before the king whose hand is to be laid upon him in honour.

Is the shepherd not joyful beneath his trembling, that he shall wear the mark of the king?

Yet is he not more mindful of his trembling?

For what is it to die but to stand naked in the wind and to melt into the sun?

And what is it to cease breathing, but to free the breath from its restless tides, that it may rise and expand and seek God unencumbered?

Only when you drink from the river of silence shall you indeed sing.

And when you have reached the mountain top, then you shall begin to climb

.And when the earth shall claim your limbs, then shall you truly dance.

From the Night   Henry Vaughan (1621- 1695)

There is in God (some say)
A deep, but dazzling darkness; as men here
Say it is late and dusky, because they
See not all clear;
O for that night! where I in him
Might live invisible and dim.

Mist   Laurie Mueller ©

The mist rises over
The coming in
And the going out of the ocean
I sit at my window
And watch the majesty of nature
And I realize
That the memory of you
Will not pass away so easily
As the morning mist
I, but a moment ago saw.

*Sometimes when one person is missing, the whole world
seems depopulated.*   Alphonse De Lamarantine (1790-
1869)

Only a Little While   Yakamochi (c. 716-785)

We were together
Only a little while,
And we believed our love
Would last a thousand years.

An Updated Version of Funeral Blues - Laurie Mueller ©

Stop the clocks!
Turn off the computers!
Put away your iPhones!
Park the cars!
Make the neon signs go dark!
You have died
And I want to turn off the world
and only feel my deep sorrow for you –

The pain that sears through my heart and into my very core
The pain that encompasses every fibre of my being and
saps every bit of my energy in my body, in my soul and in
my spirit –

Oh how you would scoff at my grief.
You would tell me to take the dog for a walk
Oh how you would scoff at my grief.
You would tell me to take the dog for a walk
Answer my email and phone another friend.
You would tell me to celebrate life
And rejoice for having known you
You would encourage me to go on.
And for you… just for you… and perhaps for me….I
will….eventually listen to your silent words.

The world is full of lonely people,
Each isolated in a private, secret dungeon.
                                    --Loretta Girzartis

No!   Laurie Mueller ©

No funeral gloom, no memorial tears, no wailing, no
gnashing of teeth when I am gone
Because I will only seem to be gone
But I will not be far away.

No long speeches… no black mourning clothes, no
graveyard grimness

Instead put on your bright colored clothes
And sing praises
And sing songs of joy
And remember me with gladness.

To Those I Love   Isla Paschal Richardson (1886-1971)

If I should ever leave you,
Whom I love
To go along the silent way. . .
Grieve not.
Nor speak of me with tears.
But laugh and talk of me
As if I were beside you there.

(I'd come...I'd come,
Could I but find a way!
But would not tears and
And grief be barriers?)

And when you hear a song
Or see a bird I loved,
Please do not let the thought of me

134

Be sad...for I am loving you
Just as I always have...

You were so good to me!
There are so many things
I wanted still to do...
So many things I wanted to say
to you...Remember that
I did not fear...It was
Just leaving you
That was so hard to face.

We cannot see beyond...
But this I know:
I loved you so...
'twas heaven here with you!

Early Death   Hartley Coleridge (1796-1849)

She pass'd away like morning dew
Before the sun was high;
So brief her time, she scarcely knew
The meaning of a sigh.

As round the rose its soft perfume,
Sweet love around her floated;
Admired she grew—while mortal doom
Crept on, unfear'd, unnoted.

Love was her guardian Angel here,
But Love to Death resign'd her;
Tho' Love was kind, why should we fear
But holy Death is kinder?

Unfinished Laurie Mueller ©

How empty seems the city
      Since you have gone.

Unfamiliar faces, long lonely streets
Homes with the porch lights turned out
And the curtains drawn.
Coffee shops with closed signs on their windows.

Construction sites with lonely cranes hanging over head
and standing still. No one to operate them.
Empty yards. No workers there.

The sun comes up and the sun goes down.
The commuters travel back and forth from suburb to city.
Phones ring, emails come in, front door bells go off

But none of it has any meaning
Without your presence.

The children run and play and laugh in the school yards
and disappear into buildings
But I cannot find joy.

*When I refuse to forgive, I am burning a bridge that
someday I will need to pass over.*   Josh McDowell

*No man is an island, entire of itself; every man is a piece of
the continent.*   John Donne (1572-1631)

*Everyone has a right to his own opinion. It's generally no
use to anyone else.* (Anon)

This Doesn't Count (Anon)

Old Bill was dying. With time running out, he wanted to make things right with his friend Harry. Once best friends, Bill knew their relationship was presently at odds. Bill had often challenged Harry on trivial matters, and in recent months, they hadn't spoken at all. Sincerely wanting to resolve the problem, Bill sent for Harry.

When Harry arrived at Bill's hospital bed, Bill apologized for his role in hurting their relationship. Bill said he was afraid of entering eternity with bad feelings between them, and he wanted to make things right before he died. Then he reached out for Harry's hand and said, "I forgive you. Will you please forgive me?" What joy that brought to Harry, and he agreed forgiveness was in order.

Just as Harry was leaving, however, old Bill shouted after him, "But remember, if I don't die and somehow get better, this doesn't count!"

We make a living by what we get; we make a life by what we give. Duane Hulse (1921-2003)

It isn't a song until it's sung
It isn't a bell until it's rung
It isn't love until it's given away.
(Anon)

To live in hearts we leave behind is not to die. Thomas Campbell (1777-1844)

From Romeo and Juliet   William Shakespeare (1564-1616)

Act III Scene II
…when he shall die,
Take him and cut him out in little stars,
And he will make the face of heaven so fine
That all the world will be in love with night
And pay no worship to the garish sun.

Psalm 23

The Lord is my shepherd; I shall not want.

He makes me to lie down in green pastures: he leads me beside the still waters.

He restores my soul: he leads me in the paths of righteousness for his name's sake.

Yea, though I walk through the valley of the shadow of death; I will fear no evil: for you art with me; my rod and my staff to comfort me.

You prepare a table before me in the presence of my enemies: you anoint my head with oil; my cup runs over.

Surely goodness and mercy shall follow me all the days of my life; and I will dwell in the house of the Lord forever.

What my tongue dares not that my heart shall say.   William Shakespeare (1564-1616)

Ecclesiastes 3:1-9 (New International Version)
A Time for Everything

There is a time for everything,
 and a season for every activity under heaven:

2 a time to be born and a time to die,
 a time to plant and a time to uproot,

3 a time to kill and a time to heal,
 a time to tear down and a time to build,

4 a time to weep and a time to laugh,
 a time to mourn and a time to dance,

5 a time to scatter stones and a time to gather them,
 a time to embrace and a time to refrain,

6 a time to search and a time to give up,
 a time to keep and a time to throw away,

7 a time to tear and a time to mend,
 a time to be silent and a time to speak,

8 a time to love and a time to hate,
 a time for war and a time for peace.

9 What does the worker gain from his toil?

The great use of life is to spend it for something that outlasts it. William James (1842-1910)

1 Corinthians 13 (New International Version)

[1]If I speak in the tongues of men and of angels, but have not love, I am only a resounding gong or a clanging cymbal. [2]If I have the gift of prophecy and can fathom all mysteries and all knowledge, and if I have a faith that can move mountains, but have not love, I am nothing. [3]If I give all I possess to the poor and surrender my body to the flames, but have not love, I gain nothing.

[4]Love is patient, love is kind. It does not envy, it does not boast, it is not proud. [5]It is not rude, it is not self-seeking, it is not easily angered, it keeps no record of wrongs. [6]Love does not delight in evil but rejoices with the truth. [7]It always protects, always trusts, always hopes, always perseveres.

[8]Love never fails. But where there are prophecies, they will cease; where there are tongues, they will be stilled; where there is knowledge, it will pass away. [9]For we know in part and we prophesy in part, [10]but when perfection comes, the imperfect disappears. [11]When I was a child, I talked like a child, I thought like a child, I reasoned like a child. When I became a man, I put childish ways behind me. [12]Now we see but a poor reflection as in a mirror; then we shall see face to face. Now I know in part; then I shall know fully, even as I am fully known.

[13]And now these three remain: faith, hope and love. But the greatest of these is love.

While we are mourning the loss of our friend, others are rejoicing to meet him behind the veil.   John Taylor (1753-1824)

In the night of death, hope sees a star, and listening love can hear the rustle of a wing.   Robert Ingersoll (1833-1899)

Life is eternal, and love is immortal, and death is only a horizon; and a horizon is nothing save the limit of our sight.   Rossiter Worthington Raymond (1840-1918)

Dear Mother Earth!

I think I have always specially belonged to you.

I have loved from babyhood to roll upon you, to lie with my face pressed right down on to you in my sorrows.

I love the look of you and the smell of you and the feel of you.

When I die I should like to be in you uncoffined, unshrouded, the petals of flowers against my flesh and you covering me up."   (Emily Carr, 1871-1945, from her gravestone at Ross Bay Cemetery, Victoria BC)

Chapter 8: Funeral Etiquette

*Always go to other people's funeral
otherwise they won't come to yours.*
Yogi Berra

General Courtesies

Common sense goes a long way here, and this list will give you additional pointers to help everything go smoothly for you.

1.   Arrive at the funeral home or church at least 10 minutes before the service is scheduled to begin. It is considered rude to enter the service room or chapel after the service has begun.

2.   If you arrive early, do not try to meet or speak with bereaved family members.

3.   Conversation in the chapel or church, prior to the service, is permissible, but you should be respectful of others. A friend can be greeted with a nod and a smile but conducting animated conversations should be done with discretion.

4.   Turn off your cell phone, pagers, etc. If you are on call and must wait for a call, use the vibrate feature and sit at the very back of the room.

5.	Allow family and close friends to sit at the front; business acquaintances and those who were not as close should sit farther back in the room.

6.	Do not eat, drink or chew gum during the service.

7.	Do not stare at the bereaved.

8.	Listen respectfully to those who are speaking. Do not converse with your neighbor during the service.

9.	If children become unruly, take them outside until they are calm or until the reception. Although you do not want to disrupt the service, you also do not want to deprive children of the experience. Some churches have quiet rooms in which you can go with your children.

10.	Do not send flowers to Orthodox Jews and check before sending them to Reform Jews. Instead send kosher food.

11.	Do not send flowers to Chinese after a funeral as they are a symbol of death.

12.	Write your name clearly in the guest book so that it can be read. Include a note about how you know the deceased.

13.	Viewing the deceased in an open casket is not mandatory; however, it is customary to show your respect by viewing and spending a few moments in silent prayer.

14. In receiving line, you may clasp hands, hug, or simply say these words of condolence which can express sympathy, such as: "I'm sorry." "My sympathy to you." "It was good to know Tim". "Bob was a fine person and a friend of mine. I'll miss him." "My sympathy to your mother."

15. If you are a member of the Receiving Line you may simply say: "Thanks for coming." "John talked about you often." "I didn't realize so many people cared." "Come see me when you can." It is very appropriate to tell a story about the deceased that you experienced. Remember to make it about them and not about you. An example: "I always appreciated meeting Bev at church. She always had a hug and a kind word to say. She often wore her red blazer and look smashing in it. Every Sunday she brought her grandchildren to church and was so proud of them. I can still see Suzi rushing back to Grandma to get her collection money and then rushing down the aisle to catch up with the other children. It was a pleasure getting to know them all. Bev will be greatly missed."

16. If you are attending a graveside service: As soon as you have parked your car in the cemetery, move as quickly as possible to the graveside. Do not attempt to engage the immediate family in conversation either

before or immediately after the graveside service. It is courteous to follow, rather than precede, the family when returning to your car.

Clothing

Queen Victoria was widowed in 1861 and then continued to dress in black until her death in 1901. We do not have such customs today even though some of us look great in black!

1. You do not need to wear black, however you do need to dress tastefully as you would attending any important event such as a job interview or a graduation service. Shorts are not acceptable and jeans should be chosen only if you have nothing else.

2. Your dress should be appropriately conservative and respectful for the family and others in attendance. Most men choose formal clothes like a suit, and would normally wear a black tie if they have one.

3. Don't show too much cleavage.

4. Some churches require head coverings; if you are unsure, take a scarf with you in case it is needed.

Before and After the Service

1. Close friends and family may choose to drop by the home (a phone call first is recommended) and offer

condolences and often bring food. It is also a time when other services can be offered. Check with others around the grieving to see what needs to be done.

2. Telephoning a family member gives you an opportunity to offer your services and make them feel you really care. If they wish to discuss their recent loss, don't hesitate to talk to the person about the deceased. Be a good listener.

3. A personal note of sympathy or a card is very meaningful. Express yourself openly and sincerely. An expression such as "I'm sorry to learn of your loss" is welcomed by the family and can be kept with other messages.

4. In some cases, it is customary for friends to call at the funeral home prior to the day of the funeral service. A "friend" could include co-workers and some of the deceased's superiors.

5. If an employee loses a very close relative, such as a husband, wife, father or mother, the immediate superior should call at the funeral home or send appropriate sympathy wishes.

6. When sending memorial gifts, be certain to mention that the gift is being made in memory of the deceased. The organization receiving the gift will normally send a list of donors to the family so the family can express its thanks and acknowledge the donation.

7.   If you are sick with a cold, flu or other contagious disease, stay at home and send your regrets.

Words for Thank You Letters

It is difficult to put my thoughts into words, but I want you to know how much I appreciate your kind and helpful words and deeds over these past few weeks.

Thanks so much for the flowers! We thought that all the floral offerings were lovely and that your basket of red roses was especially beautiful. Again, our thanks for an expression of friendship we shall never forget.

Both Harry and I wish to thank you most sincerely for serving as a pallbearer. At such a difficult time, one appreciates the true meaning of friendship.

Your letter of condolence was a source of strength. I wish I could express myself as well in attempting to thank you for your expression of sympathy. The knowledge that we have such sympathetic and understanding friends is of immeasurable value at such a time.

Everyone agreed that your baked ham and tomato aspic was delicious. We can't thank you enough for your thoughtfulness -- so typical of you! No one knows how precious true friendship is until they have been through such an experience.

Chapter 9: Dealing with Difficult People at the Funeral

*Be kind and gentle to one another. Set
pride and ego aside, it has no place here.
Compromise when necessary and make
this goodbye the best one you can give.*

Bill Jenkins

Family differences will not magically be dissolved because a loved one has died. In some cases people will work together to get through the situation, but in other families trying to work together will only acerbate the stress and strain that has been felt before. Bring your support system into use during this time. If there is a family member that you think you can't communicate with, perhaps it would be best to work through a person that you both know and trust. You might also consider a clergy person or the funeral director to be the communicator.

Some of the horror stories I have heard involve people who fit this description:

- Relatives who don't get along with one another
- Disenfranchised children of the deceased
- Family members who wanted something different to happen at the funeral
- Family members who think that there was favoritism in the family

- Family members, including ex-spouses or ex-in-laws, who want to control the event
- Control freaks

This person may use disrespectful language and actions to try to make you feel intimidated or inferior. This person may blame you for past actions or things that have gone wrong. They may ignore you. They may spread stories about you to others and yet smile and act friendly to your face.

Here are some techniques to get along with those difficult people, if only for the few minutes that you will have to interact with them at the funeral or at the reception afterwards.

Recommendation #1

Be realistic about your relationship. Don't obsess about them. Don't expect miracles. Don't take the conflict personally. Realize that there could be many other factors that have caused this friction and uneasiness to exist.

Recommendation #2

Have a positive and unflappable attitude. Think about 3 things that you do like or could like about them. Focus on their strong positive points. Be friendly, self-confident and calm. Be compassionate when you are talking with them.

Recommendation #3

Isolate the problem and understand that the behavior is the problem and not the person. It is important to deal with the problem and not get into name calling or character defamation.

Recommendation #4

Be prepared for them. Have a mental conversation with them. Practice in your head – before you see them – of conversations in which the two of you are communicating and getting along.

Recommendation #5

Make a point to speak to this individual. Say hello and make a comment about the deceased if possible. Don't worry if they don't respond. Don't take the bait. Don't argue. Don't become emotional.

Recommendation #6

Don't fight back – educate them about the reasons that you had chosen to do what it is you doing (whether it be the hymns that are chosen, the color of the flowers or the place where your loved one is being buried). Be open to their feedback.

If you don't have to deal with this person or people, stay as far away from them as possible. Don't feel that you have to engage them in conversation.

Have a receiving line in a spot that doesn't create traffic congestion and where people can choose whether they want to participate or not without looking awkward.

Think Like an Adult

Transactional Analysis gives us another helpful view of how we often react to situations and gives some suggestions for more effective ways. When a person tells you what to do (as a critical parent might tell a child) you may often react in the way that a child would react. This can lead to an unhealthy dialogue. If, instead, you take a moment to think about the statement and how to respond in an "adult" way you can often diffuse the moment. Here are some examples:

Example #1:

Difficult Person says: *You should sing more hymns in the service.*

Unhelpful response: *No! We're not going to ... stop telling me what to do.*

Adult-driven response: *Yes, we thought about that and had to make some decisions around the timing. We wanted to*

152

have two speakers and three readings. Therefore we chose only to have 2 hymns so that the timing wasn't too much for some people.

Example #2

Difficult Person says: *You should have Aunt Jane give the eulogy.*

Unhelpful response: *Why do you always have to want something different than what we decided?*

Adult-driven response: *That is a great idea and one that we thought of. However, Ken offered and he has stories from Aunt Jane. He's really excited about doing this.*

Example #3

Difficult Person says: *You should not have used these green tea cups with the mauve table cloths. It clashes and looks terrible. You had better change them before people get here.*

Unhelpful response: *Oh stop picking on everything we do.*

Adult-driven response: *They do look rather garish; however, Aunt Mildred set the tables and thought that it would be a perfect tribute for her sister. We decided to honor her wishes. This may be one of the last 'tea parties' that she hosts.*

Chapter 10: In Memoriam – One Year Later

Fill your paper with the breathing of the heart.
William Wordsworth

Remembering your loved one on the anniversary of the death is a part of a healthy, normal grieving process. There are many ways to acknowledge the anniversary of the death of a loved one; some examples include sharing a special family dinner, going to a special place that you shared together, or creating a painting or song.

You might send a plant or flowers to the family, have them placed on the altar of your church of worship, or donate to a special charity.

One woman I know sends a flowering plant to her deceased husband's parents each year.

Another person sent a flower arrangement on the anniversary of her husband's death to the friend who stayed with her throughout the 10-day search for her husband's downed plane. In this case it was a thank you and a remembrance.

One way that is sometimes chosen is to place an "In Memoriam" notice in your local newspaper. It is found in the section following the Obituary Columns in the newspaper. There is also a section on the Memorial Websites for Anniversary notices.

An "In Memoriam" can have a picture of the deceased, dates of their birth and death and a special message. The special message can consist of a poem, some prose, or a message that you would say if you could speak to them at this time. At the end of the notice, the names of the submitting friends or relatives are noted. Last names are not necessary. In some cases, "Your loving family" is enough.

Sample "In Memoriam" Notices (adapted from the local newspaper.)

In Memoriam

Tina Louise Sinclair
February 28, 1995 – July 12, 2019
Life is a gift! You were a gift!
We look forward to the time
we are together again.
With everlasting love from your family.

xxx

Robert Potvin
1949 – 2008
It has been a year since you passed away and we think of you constantly. Thankfully, your suffering is ended, but our pain of losing you continues.

We miss you every day.

Love from your wife and children.

McLeod, Rita

December 15, 1935 – May 22, 2008

I feel your gentle spirit today as every day I am blessed to have such a loving and wonderful mother. Missing you.

Your loving daughter, Lisa

xxx

In Memoriam

To my wife – Winnifred Alisand Leckie

September 23, 1953 – June 1, 2003

I hold it true, whate'er befall;
I feel it when I sorrow most;
'Tis better to have loved and lost
Than never to have loved at all.
(Alfred Lord Tennyson)

I will love you always…Jack

xxx

Gresham, Dorothy (1920 – 2008)

It has been a year since you left us.

We greatly miss your hearty laugh, strong spirit and kind ways.

But we know you have "crossed the bar" into a better place just as Tennyson wrote in one of your favorite poems:

Sunset and evening star,
And one clear call for me!
And may there be no moaning of the bar,
When I put out to sea,
But such a tide as moving seems asleep,
Too full for sound and foam,
When that which drew from out the boundless deep
Turns again home.
Twilight and evening bell,
And after that the dark!
And may there be no sadness of farewell,
When I embark;
For tho' from out our bourne of Time and Place
The flood may bear me far,
I hope to see my Pilot face to face
When I have crost the bar.

Remembering you, dear Dorothy, with love,
From Jennifer & all your dear friends

Chapter 11: Planning for Your Own Funeral

"I hate funerals and would not attend my own if it could be avoided, but it is well for every person to stop once in a while to think of what sort of a collection of mourners they are training for their final event."
Adapted from Robert T. Morris

Introduction

When I started to think about pre-planning, I contacted a Funeral Home and Memorial Gardens representative at our local Home Show one spring weekend. My husband and I chatted with the representatives and they promised to call us the following week. Both phone calls were returned promptly on the day promised. We set up appointments and met with both. We chose to visit them at their site because we wanted to actually see what they had to offer. We could have chosen to have the representatives come to our home at our convenience.

I asked the first representative if she made a lot of appointments from being at the Home Show. She grimaced and said, "You were actually the friendliest people I talked to all day. Most people just hurried on by!"

Many people don't want to think about their own death. Are they afraid it will bring their death on sooner if they think, talk or plan for it? That is what Professor Eric Dolansky of Brock University calls magical thinking. "Magical thinking is the idea that two rationally unrelated events are related." (2009, Marr)

Once you have been through the stress of a loved one's death, perhaps it will make it easier for you to think about pre-arranging the details for yourself. Remember it will make it easier for those left behind.

If you choose to pre-plan, perhaps this guide will give you some information that will help you to begin the process.

Preparation

What do you need to do to prepare your end of life arrangements? There are many things to think about and if you have your affairs organized and your paperwork in a safe place, which your relatives can easily find, you will be doing them a great service.

Certain items are important for you to have in place:

1. A will. A lawyer is always a good idea when preparing your will. In some areas, it is not legally binding without their seal.

2. A Power of Attorney (this applies to any situation in which you become incapacitated. It will allow people who you trust to make decisions for you in such cases

as if you were in a coma or acquired Alzheimer's disease.)

3. A legal document (sometimes called a living will and a health care directive) that gives instructions about your end-of-life choices for health care when you can no longer transmit those desires due to such things as a coma, Alzheimer's disease, etc. See below for more details.

4. Organ Donation. This must be arranged before you die. Check with your local authorities to register. Let your family know you have done this.

5. A file with a list of items such as your life and other insurance policies, agreements with funeral homes including funeral/cremation documentation and certificate of entitlement of cemetery property, the name of your lawyer and accountant, birth certificate, marriage certificate, mortgage papers, financial records, house deeds, automobile information and documents, citizenship papers, military discharge papers, and other important documents and valuables.

6. A document with any last wishes that you would like for your memorialization such as hymns sung or minister you would like to perform the service.

Items 1 – 4 will vary depending on the country and region in which you live. Check with your local authorities and professionals to get the correct advice for you.

Things to think about for final days

Wills allow your worldly possessions to be easily transferred to your heirs with the least amount of trouble. Those who die intestate (without a will) pay extra taxes for the privilege of having the government coordinate the disbursement of assets. Check with authorities in your local area to find out whether or not you need a lawyer to file your will. In some places a handwritten, witnessed statement is legal while in other areas it must be notarized by an official such as a notary public or a lawyer.

At the same time that you make your will you can appoint a **Power of Attorney,** which is the person(s) who will look after your financial and property affairs if you become incapacitated and unable to communicate your wishes. It can sometimes, but not always, include health matters. This document must be notarized.

Health Directives and Living Wills

A **Health Directive** is a document which you create and sign that appoints someone to make decisions about your health or personal care if you become unable to make those decisions for yourself because of loss of capacity. It covers such areas as medication, diet, exercise, dental care, mental health and other normal health care needs.

A **Living Will** is a type of advance directive that usually addresses end-of-life treatment choices in general terms such as the medical treatment you do or do not want administered during a terminal illness. These documents help family members make tough decisions easier. You can consult with your family doctor or community nurse on these issues. Again, check with your area of the country you live in to find out what is legal and what is not. For instance, in Canada nine out of our ten provinces have passed laws that allow people to make directives in which they can legally appoint a substitute decision maker and give binding instructions on how decisions regarding health care are to be made.

It is very important that once you have decided and created these documents that you let your family and decision makers know that they exist and where they are kept. Inform your family doctor.

Planning Your Final Arrangements

You don't have to leave the planning of your final arrangements to others. You can have it arranged ahead of time. Representatives from funeral homes and memorial societies will meet with you and discuss the options and help you create a plan. This planning can also include payment for future service. There are several advantages to this. You are getting what you want. There is less for grieving relatives to figure out after you are gone. If you prepay your funeral it will cost you present-day rates as opposed to the possible increased rates at the time of your death. The sales folk are very helpful; however, you must remember that they are selling a product. Be sure to check out a few before making a decision. In this type of planning, you will want to decide:

- What type of service and final rites do you want?
- Do you want to be buried?
- Do you want to be cremated?
- Where do you want your final remains to rest?

It would be wise for you to review the checklist of "What to do When a Person Dies" and make sure that your personal papers are organized and easy for your survivors to find. Keep the list in a safe place such as a home safe or safety deposit box at the bank.

Cremation

Depending on the part of the world that you live in the statistics of cremation or burial today will vary. In Canada more people on the West Coast (70%) are choosing cremation over burial. On the east Coast burial is the higher statistic making the Canadian average around 49% in recent years. (Encyclopedia of Cremation Edited by Douglas J. Davies with Lewis H. Mates) In the United Kingdom since 2001, statistics show that 75% of deaths have been cremated. (Office for National Statistics, the Office of the General Register of Scotland and the Northern Ireland Statistics and Research Agency) In the United States in 2005, 30.88% of the deaths were cremated.

Roman Catholics are now able to choose cremation (Canon 176 §3). *The Church earnestly recommends that the pious custom of burying the bodies of the deceased be observed; nevertheless, the Church does not prohibit cremation unless it was chosen for reasons contrary to Christian doctrine* (Roman Catholic Church 1983). It would be best to check with your local priest for his suggestions in this matter.

The Funeral or Memorial Service

Some people plan their funeral service. My grandmother, who was a church organist, had her music picked out. You can leave some suggestions but remember that this final service is to help those left behind. Some of their healing comes in the preparation of the final tribute. My suggestion is that you leave some instructions and allow them to create the rest. For instance, I have determined that I want to be cremated and that my ashes be placed with my parents' remains. I have written it into my will. I have also left a file of stories that my family may or may not use in the "Celebration of Life." I have two song requests. These aren't in my will, but I've repeated the suggestion several times to my family and written it in amongst the stories. Will my family comply? That will be up to them.

Several people have told me stories of poems or inspirational writings that their loved one left for them to read after they had died. It was an act of love and one that said to the survivor, I loved you so much I left a message especially for you. For Sandy and her sister, their grandmother cut out inspirational writings and addressed them specifically to each granddaughter. For Winifred, her father left a poem that described his life and his relationships with her mother and with her. It brought her understanding and peace.

Stories for Your Eulogy

Writing the stories of your life is a nice way to leave behind your legacy and to allow others to have access to some of the more significant points in your life. Be sure to leave these where they will be found after you die and before your funeral service.

When my mother died it was easy for me to tell stories of her life for the 38 years that she had lived before I was even born because so many of them were written down. If you haven't written and published your memoirs, as most people haven't, simply putting some words to paper will help. Words on paper are probably the best way to leave these stories. When a friend of mine died in a plane crash, I offered the family a video tape of an interview that I had done with their mother. They could not bring themselves to look at it – too great was their grief and shock. Words on paper were easier to handle.

When you write your stories, do so in an informal way. Jot down your memories. Tell them in anecdotal form or even in point form. You do not need to be eloquent or a formally trained writer. Don't worry about details unless they are necessary for the impact of the story.

Another way to leave information behind is to create a timeline of your life and mention significant and interesting events. This could include educational achievements, birth of children, marriages, promotions, special trips you took, achievements of any kind, deaths of other family members. You can write stories to match or not.

Remember that this is not just about you, but about helping the grieving process of your family and friends that you are leaving behind.

Donations of Organs

You may wish to leave your body to science or certain organs to people who can use them. People of all ages may be organ and tissue donors. Popularity of this practice, as well as laws, differs from country to country. Check with your local government, medical school or coroner to find out how you can do that in your area. In British Columbia Canada we can become a donor online. The information is stored in a secure database and when a death occurs the database is automatically searched. The following information came from the BC organ donor website at: http://www.transplant.bc.ca/what_organs_can.htm#heart

These organs can be donated and used in the following ways:

1. Heart

For those suffering heart failure from a disease or virus, a donated heart makes the difference between living and dying.

2. Lungs

Donated lungs are transplanted into people suffering from fatal lung conditions, such as Cystic Fibrosis.

3. Kidneys

The two kidneys given by each donor are transplanted into two different recipients, who need only one functioning kidney to lead a normal life.

4. Liver

The liver filters the blood and metabolizes the food we eat. The only cure for liver failure is a liver transplant.

5. Pancreas

Donated to diabetics, a new pancreas eliminates the need for daily insulin injections.

Recent, breakthrough research in Canada has found a new procedure for transplanting pancreatic islet cells to cure diabetics.

6. Eye Tissue (Cornea)

When it comes to restoring lost vision, corneal transplants have a 90 to 95 per cent success rate and are among the most often performed transplants.

7. Bone

Bone that has been destroyed by tumors or infections can often be replaced with healthy donated bone, saving limbs that would otherwise have to be amputated.

8. Skin

Donated skin is used as a dressing to speed up the healing process for severe burn victims.

9. Heart Valves

Donated heart valves are often used for infants whose heart valves are defective at birth.

10. Bowel

A donated bowel is often transplanted into infants and corrects birth defects. This saves lives and improves quality of life.

11. Tendons and ligaments

Donated tendons and ligaments are used in orthopedic and plastic surgery to repair or replace tendons and ligaments that have been destroyed by disease.

12. Veins

Donated veins are used to replace and repair veins that have been destroyed by disease. Used in heart by-pass surgery.

Preplanning with a Funeral Home

At one funeral service supplier that I visited, I received a quote for services with prices. At a second place I went to, I had to ask if they could write down the prices.

Here are some of the services one organization offered:

A. Funeral Service Description:

- Internment
- Cremation
- Shipping
- Immediate Disposition

B. Professional Services and Fees

- Professional and Staff Services
- Registration and Documentation

C. Care and Preparation of the Remains:

- Preparation and Embalming
- Refrigeration
- Other Care and Preparation

D. Use of Facilities and Equipment:

- Facilities for services/visitation
- Facilities to embalm/prepare/shelter
- Other use of facilities and staff

E. Transportation

- Removal and transfer
- Funeral Coach
- Funeral lead/clergy vehicle
- Funeral Service Vehicle
- Funeral Vehicles

F. Merchandise & Other Services:

- Casket and type
- Outer Burial Container/Vault
- Urn/Vase
- Alternative Container
- 24-hour Compassionate Helpline
- Acknowledgment Cards
- Aftercare Planner
- Commemorative bookmarks
- Crematory Fee
- Everlasting Memorial
- Flowers
- Memorial Package
- Register Book
- Prayer Cards

- Service Folders
- Reception
- Reception host/ess
- Obituary Notices
- Escorts
- Certified Death Certificate Copies
- Shipping Container
- Clergy
- Musicians/Singers
- Hairdressing
- Permits

2020 ADDENDUM: A "ZOOM" Celebration of Life Service

A Zoom Celebration

You can be as creative as you want when developing a Celebration of Life on Zoom. You can easily add a photo slide show, play music from your computer or show a video. Or do all three. If you have musicians who have the right sound attachments on their computers, you can broadcast their music, or you can share music right from your computer files. You can invite others to speak from the comfort of their own home, and even show memorabilia.

Planning a Zoom Service is much like planning any other service. Have a clear plan, make sure you have helpers. If you are the host, it is very difficult to also be the technical support. These are two jobs that require full attention. Ask an experienced person to help you with the technical aspects.

Plan your program for no longer than 60 minutes. People easily tire watching and being on-line.

Free versions of Zoom time out after 45-minute sessions.

The paid program, Zoom Meetings, allows for waiting rooms, gallery view and breakout rooms, all of which are handy to create a successful event. Please note: there is another Zoom program that is Webinar. Webinar does not allow for the interaction that Zoom Meetings extends and is more suited to larger gatherings in which the speaker is highlighted.

Pay attention to the digital capabilities of your audience. Remember that not everyone uses a computer, knows how to use Zoom, lives in an area with good internet reception or has high speed internet. Some people have older computers that don't have the speed, or the size needed to have a stable connection on Zoom.

Practice ahead of time and get acquainted with the program or have someone experienced host your gathering to ensure the best possible experience for those in attendance.

You can record the service on Zoom to send out to those people who were unable to attend at the scheduled time.

Besides Zoom's updated security system, there are two other features that keep the Zoom gathering safe from unwanted guests.

Only those issued an invitation will have the meeting number and password.

There is a "waiting room" feature. Those people attending will be let into a waiting room where they will stay until the technical assistant clicks them into the on-line gathering.

Inviting Guests & Privacy Protection

How to tell people about the Zoom Celebration

Remember, because you are on-line, you can invite friends and family from around the world.

- Include the notice of a Celebration of Life in the obituary as you would any live service and include an e-mail address for family & friends to request an invitation to the event. Do not put the zoom address and password on a public site.

- You may also send email invitations of the zoom event to the people that you want to attend.

- Give a friend a phoning list to contact possible attendees then email the event link to those who said yes to the zoom invitation.

Make sure that each person receives a "Zoom" invitation at least the day before the event. If there are people attending that may be new to Zoom, be sure to give them clear directions on how to sign up for an account ahead of time or the Zoom website for them to download.

In the e-mail, you might suggest that people

- flag this e-mail for easy access on the day of the event or

- can copy and paste the information, including the meeting number and the password into their calendar so that they only need to click on the link at the appointed time. Usually, invite people to come 15 minutes before your program begins.

Privacy Issues

There are a number of ways to protect your gathering from being invaded by unwanted participants.

1. Don't publicize the zoom meeting number and password in any newspaper or other public forum.
2. Use the Waiting Room Feature in Zoom to add another layer of protection against unwanted guests. (See program roles & Software Features for more information regarding the Waiting Rooms)
3. Uninvited guests that arrive in the waiting room can be blocked from entering the main site as they can be left in the waiting room.

Program Roles

You will need to plan for a Session Leader, also known as a host, a celebrant, an officiant, a minister or a funeral director. For this tutorial, we will call this person the Host. Other folks that you can choose to participate include a eulogist, a singer, other speakers. You will also need to have one or two Zoom Technical Assistants on the job.

Host

Will you be the host, or have you asked someone else? You may choose to have a paid professional take on this role. Whether you contract with someone from a funeral home or a church, please remember that their time is worth the money you pay to have them do this.

Technical Assistant

Have a Zoom Tech person (or 2 depending on the size of your gathering) assigned that has worked with Zoom before or has taken the program for some test runs. They can then:

- Take phone calls from newbies to Zoom who can't figure out how to get on
- Have the waiting room enabled. This means that you can make sure that you know who is entering.
- Check the chat feature and follow up with anyone that needs it.
- Keep people on mute during the service and except when speaking.
- Teach people to use the Chat function.
- Have the gatekeeper/tech person watch for messages and have them alert you if something needs to be dealt with.
- Have one person appointed to keep a record of who attended. Some Pro versions have an automated

reporting system. Check your operating instructions for your program.

Planning the Program

Create your digital "program" which will be your agenda. You will find details of how to create a program in Part Two of this book.

Your Notes & Agenda

Have print copies of anything that you are doing. As one on-line presenter has been heard to say:

"If something can go wrong it will. Have print copies of everything you are doing to thwart the gremlins."

People feel more comfortable and relaxed when they know what the agenda is. You can send it out ahead of time by e-mail or verbally announce it at the beginning of the service.

Decide on the program roles and identify what equipment you will need to adequately carry out your plan. These two items are discussed in their own sections.

Planning A Photo Show

If you are planning to show photos or videos from your computer be sure to practice ahead of time and know how to use the share screen component. Have the pictres on your desktop for easy access at the correct time in your program. Practice this several times before hand. There are programs that can add music to your photos for a better experience.

Planning Music

Do you have access to friends, family members or acquaintances that can supply live music? As mentioned in another section, a professional microphone is recommended for proper sound enjoyment. This would be attached to musician's computer. If not, you can use recorded music from your computer that will play with the right sound when you have set the correct option in settings. Make sure you have enabled "Play sound from computer" and tested it ahead of time.

Practice ahead of time so that you feel comfortable. Record your practice and play it back so you can see what changes you would like to make. I have even done this just using the recorder on my computer and not on zoom.

Be prepared for Possible Interruptions

Cats love to purr and wander up for a snuggle when you are sitting still. Dogs bark and can be a sound and visual distraction. Radio and TV can also interfere with your sound quality. Keep participants on mute for these same reasons.

The Program

General Advice

1. Start on time.
2. Give them any technical details they may need at the start, such as how to:
   a. enable video
   b. mute and unmute
   c. use the chat feature,
   d. how to change the name on their screen to match who they are (not their daughter's or granddaughters but their name)
3. Use the chat feature. Invite people to write memories or greetings to the family in the chat. Schedule a time in the service when you or your technical support person will read these comments to the assembled.
4. Record your session using the Cloud or One Drive. This can be enabled in settings or on the screen menu any time during your service. The processing can take quite some time so do not expect it to be ready right away. By recording the event, you can review it later or share it with others.
5. Speak slowly and clearly. Check with the others to make sure they can hear you. If not, turn up the volume on your computer or headset.
6. You can add breakout rooms for small groups of people to have a chance to chat together.
7. Look into the camera, not onto the screen, when talking to the group. To remind you, paste two emoji

eyes on either side of the camera. Watch the eyes! The best paper notes are points written on 'recipe cards' rather than large pieces of paper to read. You don't have to be a professional to be appreciated for taking on the hosting.

Sample Opening

Welcome Statement: Good afternoon everyone, and welcome to our Celebration of Life for "name". We will have a program that will last for approximately 60 minutes.

Here are some housekeeping Details: Before getting started, I'd like to go over a few housekeeping items, so you know how to participate in today's event. At any time during the event, you will have the opportunity to type memories into the chat. Our technical support will alert me to them so that I can read them at (the end of the service or share them later or whatever you choose.) I notice that Aunt Matilda is using her grandson, Jonathan's program. Auntie, I am going to ask our technical support person to change the name on your program so that people today know your name. It is something that is easy for your grandson to put back later.

We will be recording this celebration for a few of our family members who could not attend here today.

And now, let's get started. (and you carry on with your plan.)

Sample Closing

When the service is over, and you have thanked the people for coming, end with a positive note.

This is also a good time to invite people to meet in breakout rooms (see section on break out rooms) and allow them 15 - 20 minutes (or whatever you choose) to chat with each other.

Software & Equipment Needed

Software

A Zoom Meetings Program.

Equipment

The equipment you need includes a computer that is less than 5 years old and has a working microphone, camera, and internet capabilities.

Strong Internet Connection

If you have chosen to be the host of the event, make sure your computer is hard-wired into the modem for this time.

External Microphone

Does the host and the other designated speakers have an adequate microphone to be clearly heard?

You can use a wired headset with a microphone; it is a general best practice for higher-quality audio as it often reduces background noise better than other built-in options.

Ear phones with microphone attached can work suitably for this if you don't want to spend money on an external microphone. Zoom gives you the opportunity to check your microphone before signing in. Test your sound and volume well ahead of time. Some people buy an external microphone that attaches to their computer for speaking events. If you plan to sing or play an instrument, an external mic is definitely needed. You can check your favorite tech store for an appropriate model for your needs.

Music is harder on zoom. Group singing doesn't work because only one person can be heard at a time and multiple speakers are not heard. Recorded music can work. If you have a soloist, they will require a special microphone. And knowledge of the program. Pre-recorded music can work well because it is played from within the computer system and uses a different sound system. There is a setting in Zoom that allows the computer to manage the sound and therefore allows you to share your playlists or YouTube music with good sound with your guests.

External Camera

If you are planning to show memorabilia use an attached camera that can focus on the items rather than trying to hold them up to your computer camera.

Personal Appearance

Dress

You'll be on video, dress to impress not to distract, so be sure to wear solid colors as opposed to garments with patterns. Be mindful of any accessories or jewelry if you are expressive with your hands as the noise and movement can be quite eye catching and taking away from the meaning of the service.

Sit still! Some people rock in their chair or jiggle or run their fingers through their long hair. Resist the urge as it is distracting to the guests who have come here to concentrate on their memories of the deceased.

Lighting

Make sure the host and key participants are placed in a well-lit area Be sure there is no window behind you and have an equal amount of light on both sides of your face.

Background

Have a clutter free background behind you so as not to distract from what you are saying. A plain wall is best.

On some computers you can enable a prepared background, or you can add one of your own photos to create the background. There are downsides in how this feature interacts with your image. Play with it ahead of time to see if it will work for you. Another downside for using the template background is that it is one more thing that can take the emphasis off of the main purpose of the event. Use with caution.

On-Screen Zoom Features

Gallery View vs Speaker View

Use the Gallery view so you can see the participants. Use speaker view to see the Eulogist. These two screens can be toggled back and forth. Also, if you have more than will fit on your computer screen (25 in most cases), you can hover over the left-hand side of your screen and an arrow will show up. Click that arrow to see next screen of people. Some may be repeated from the previous screen to fill the space. (If you see several people are dozing off, you may want to wrap it up quickly!)

Share Screen

It is best to let your technical assistant take control of the Share Screen and putting up anything that you want displayed in the service. The Share Screen Function allows you to show photos, videos and even documents.

Chat Feature

Again, this is a good task for the technical assistant to be in charge of. You can ask this person to explain the purpose of it at the beginning of the program. It can be used for people to send you private or public messages. It can be used for people to share memories. Have the tech assistant save the chat at the end of the service so that you and your family can read them afterwards and add them to any book that you might be making in memory. You can choose if they will be read out during the service (in place of an open mic perhaps? Or if they will just remain in chat for folks to read and you to save for later.).

Mute

This is a button that can be used by the technical assistant or the participant. You can also have it disabled in the settings so that no one can unmute themselves.

Name/Rename

If someone is using someone else's computer, the name on the screen may be someone else's name. This can easily be changed by the participant or the tech assistant in the rename function. If the tech assistant makes the change, it will only stay in for the length of this session and will revert back to the original name for the next Zoom session.

Waiting Rooms

When a person first logs into the zoom meeting, you can choose that they are placed into a waiting room. The technical assistant will then let them in as they check them off the list. This is a safety as well as an organizing tool. If someone arrived into the waiting room that was not on the list, and appeared to have other intentions, the technical assistant can just leave them in the waiting room. Also, the guests arrive into the main event in an orderly form and not all springing up at once. As mentioned earlier, this is a safety feature well worth considering.

Breakout Rooms

At an appointed time, you can choose to put your guests into small groups, called breakout rooms to chat and share remembrances. You can think of these small groups as table groups that might form at the reception time after a service. You can choose how many people you want to put in each group. Six or seven people might be a number you choose if you are not sure.

The Zoom program can have up to 50 breakout rooms, so you have lots of latitude in your numbering.

You can choose to split the guests into break out rooms automatically or manually. You can allow guests to select and enter breakout rooms as they please. Some ideas for choosing groups could be family members, neighbours, work associates, interest/hobby groups.

You, as the host, can switch between sessions at any time. Check with the on-line tutorials for instructions.

One Final Comment

There are many tutorials on the Zoom site and elsewhere. The program is very user friendly. You don't have to be perfect and with the basic skills you will feel confident that you were able to give your loved one a caring 'send off,' as well as allowing a space for friends and family to 'be together' to say good-bye.

Acknowledgements

Thank you to all those people who have helped me through the researching and writing of this Guide. For years I have been attending funerals and memorial services (most always forgetting to take Kleenex with me!) of people I have loved and cared about. I have spent time with family and relatives as they experienced the trauma of losing someone close to them. This guide is my offering to help those of you who are all of a sudden burdened with a loss and honored with the task of eulogizing your loved one. Let my experience help you to do what you need to do.

As well as all those quoted throughout the book, I would also like to say **Thank You** to *Christine Nicholls*, our weekly walks and talks have inspired and motivated me and you have taught me so much about how the internet works. *Charlie Ritchie*, who would think that a 50-something woman would have a 20-something mentor! You are awesome, Charlie! *Sandy Gerbrecht*, my editor extraordinaire. Not only do you do a fabulous job, I always feel great having been in your company. *Pat Nichol*, the grand diva of inspiration and motivation. Wasn't I lucky that first day I met you in that bookstore? The women of my *Wise Women Group* – for your support and love. And to my 2020 Business Manager, *Mame McCrea*, who helped me get this all together again and out to those of you who can use it. And to my husband, *Helmuth Mueller*, for your enthusiastic support and love. I am blessed to have you with me every day!

190

About the Author

Laurie has been in the business of helping people all of her adult life. Retired from the position of Executive Director of a non-profit seniors' residence, Laurie combines her knowledge & skills to help others develop quality lifestyles for themselves and others.

Over the past 12 years, Laurie has designed and facilitated many Celebrations of Life for both clients and friends. She has led workshops on the topic and consulted with those who needed 'a little help' to get things organized.

Her skills include managing large busy industrial companies and providing consulting to a variety of sectors. She has developed and facilitated many spiritual and personal development programs as well as acting in a lay leadership role conducting weddings, worship services and study groups.

Among her other accomplishments, Laurie holds a Master's Degree from Simon Fraser University, a Counselling Certificate from the William Glasser Institute, Myers-Briggs Certification and Diplomas in Adult Education Practices.

191

Works Cited

(2002). A checklist: What to do when a relative dies. Retrieved May 23, 2009, from MFS Heritage Planning Web site: http://www.memberbenefits.com/fsga/forms/HeritagePlanning/LIFErelativedies.pdf)

(2004). Funeral information: Funeral services>Etiquette. Retrieved May 23, 2009, from Golden Rule Web site: http://www.golden-rule.com/fi-etiquette.php

(2006). Pallbearers - Funeral etiquette. Retrieved May 4, 2009, from Jacobs-French School of Knowledge Web site: http://www.a-to-z-of-manners-and-etiquette.com/pallbearers.html

(2008). Funeral etiquette. Retrieved May 23, 2009, from Speers Funeral & Cremation Services Web site: http://www.speersfuneralchapel.com/Funeral_Etiquette_-75367.html

(2009). Funeral Pall. Retrieved May 24, 2009, from The Lutheran Church Missouri Synod Web site: http://www.lcms.org/pages/internal.asp?NavID=3932

(2009). In *Merriam-Webster Online* [Web]. Merriam-Webster, Incorporated. Retrieved May 23, 2009, from http://www.merriam-webster.com/

(2009). Pre-arrangement issues. Retrieved May 23, 2009, from Speers Funeral & Cremation Services Web site: http://www.speersfuneralchapel.com/prearrangement_issues.html

(2009, February 9). Progress of cremation in the United Kingdom 1885-2007. Retrieved May 2, 2009, from Cremation Society of G.B. Web site: http://www.srgw.demon.co.uk/CremSoc4/Stats/National/ProgressF.html

(2009, January 27). National Statistics. Retrieved May 24, 2009, from Office For National Statistics Web site: http://www.statistics.gov.uk/cci/nugget.asp?id=1092

Ashenburg, Katherine (2002). *The mourner's dance: What we do when people die*. Toronto, Ontario: Macfarlane, Walter & Ross.

Balmer, Emma (2009). What pallbearers do. Retrieved May 23, 2009, from HubPages Web site: http://hubpages.com/hub/What-Pallbearers-Do

Burch, Kevin (2006). *A eulogy to remember in six simple steps*. Bath, England: Empowering Publications.

Carter, Tom (2006). *Living wills kit: Everything you need to write a living will, a representation agreement, or a health-care directive*. Brampton, Ontario: Self-Counsel Press.

Davies, Douglas J., & Mates, Lewis H. (Eds.) (2005). *Encyclopedia of Cremation*. U.K.: Durham University.

Emerson, Sally (Ed.) (2004). *In loving memory: A collection for memorial services, funerals and just getting by*. Great Britain: Little, Brown.

First Memorial Funeral Services. (2002). *Personal Planning Guide*

Jenkins, Bill (1999). How to help a friend in grief. Retrieved May 28, 2009, from Will's World Web site: http://www.willsworld.com/helpfriend.htm

Jenkins, Bill (1999). Men and women in grief. Retrieved May 8, 2009, from Will's World Web site: http://www.willsworld.com/checklist.htm

Jenkins, Bill (1999). The checklist. Retrieved May 4, 2009, from Will's World Web site: http://www.willsworld.com/checklist.htm

Jenkins, Bill (1999). What to do when the police leave: A guide to the first days of traumatic loss (Excerpts from the book). Retrieved May 23, 2009, from Will's World Web site: http://www.willsworld.com/excerpts.htm

Marr, Garry (2009, May 23). Indemnity of magical thinking. *Times-Colonist*, p. B4.

McFarlane, Doreen M. (2008). *A handbook for pastors: Funerals with today's family in mind*. Cleveland, Ohio: Pilgrim Press.

Metcalfe, Gayden, & Hays, Charlotte (2005). *Being dead is no excuse: The official southern ladies guide to hosting the perfect funeral*. New York, New York: Miramax Books.

Newland & Associates, (2002, June). Checklist: What to do when someone dies. Retrieved May 23, 2009, from UncleFed's Tax Board Web site: http://www.unclefed.com/AuthorsRow/Newland/pass_on.html

Pallbearer. (2009). In *Wikipedia* [Web]. USA: Wikimedia Foundation. Retrieved April 15, 2009, from http://en.wikipedia.org/wiki/Pallbearer

Proudfoot, Shannon (2009, May 17). Society's obsession with youth spills into obituaries. *Times -Colonist*, p. A11.

Retrieved May 2, 2009, from BibleGateway.com Web site: http://www.biblegateway.com/

Roman Catholic Church, (2003, November 4). Code of canon law. Retrieved May 23, 2009, from Vatican Archives Web site:

http://www.vatican.va/archive/ENG1104/__P4A.H
TM

Smith Ross, Judy (2004). *Good grief, I have a funeral to plan: A detailed guide to planning a funeral* . Thornbury, Ontario: Valley Girls Publishing.

Sympathy quotes. Retrieved May 15, 2009, from Sympathy Sayings Web site: http://www.sympathy-sayings.com/quotes-and-sayings/sympathy-quotes/

Takeuchi Cullen, Lisa (2003, July 7). What a way to go. Retrieved May 12, 2009, from Time Web site: http://www.time.com/time/magazine/article/0,9171, 1005160,00.html

Transporting the deceased. Retrieved May 23, 2009, from Transportation Security Administration: For Travelers Web site: http://www.tsa.gov/travelers/airtravel/specialneeds/ editorial_1296.shtm

Van Ekeren, Glenn (Ed.) (1988). *The speaker's sourcebook: Quotes, stories, and anecdotes for every occasion*. New Jersey: Prentice Hall.

Washington, Peter (Ed.) (1998). *Poems of mourning*. Toronto, Ontario: Alfred A. Knopf.

Williams Bushey, Elizabeth (2008, April 14). How to write an obituary. Retrieved April 4, 2009, from eHow Web site:

http://www.ehow.com/how_2263231_write-an-obituary.html

Wolowiec, Jeffrey (1998). Funerals. Retrieved May 10, 2009, from Family Estate Web site: http://familyestate.com/main/funeral.html

Printed in Great Britain
by Amazon

76044847R00122